TOWARD
THE RISING SUN

BY

WILLIAM GAYLEY SIMPSON

With a biographical sketch by

JEROME DAVIS

ISBN: 978-0-578-01851-5

TO ALL HUMAN LIFE

THAT MANY WHO SEE MAY COME TO SEE YET FARTHER

AND HAVE MORE STRENGTH TO UNFOLD

ACCORDING TO THE BENT AND DIRECTION

THAT ARE WITHIN THEMSELVES

Contents

WILLIAM GAYLEY SIMPSON *

AMERICA is a land of action. Men are practical, and theories to receive social recognition must be translated into deeds so that all can see results. The United States has hardly produced any great prophets or individual mystics who have sacrificed everything they had in order to clothe their highest vision in their own flesh and blood. Perhaps it is not without significance that in the first half of the twentieth century we should find amongst us a man who, in his quest for truth and his determination to put his deepest insights and his surest convictions into practice, has not only broken resolutely with conformity to things as they are but has refused to worship at the shrine of achievement even when it is idealized as unselfish service.

Bill Simpson, as he has come to be known, is an American mystic who, whatever else may be said for or against him, has tried to follow the gleam of truth and inner conviction regardless of consequences. For him it is not enough to see: it is equally necessary to do what one sees. It is not enough to dream dreams and to see visions: it is equally necessary to struggle to make those dreams come true and to realize those visions on earth. And he challenges the reality and the value of any alleged service

* In the narrative parts of the following biographical sketch, I have tried as far as possible to use Bill Simpson's own words, that the reader may get a truer picture of the man and his spirit

to humanity for the sake of which a man has to violate his integrity. He would say with Emerson:

He that feeds men serveth few,
He serves all who dares to be true.

Bill Simpson, the oldest of three children, was born July 23rd, 1892, in Elizabeth, New Jersey. Almost entirely of Gaelic ancestry, he traces back on his mother's side to hardy yeomen stock and on his father's through a long line of scholars, schoolmasters, and ministers.

His early home-life seems to have been almost perfect. It was held up in many circles as the ideal. Often he himself has declared that he looked back upon it as the Kingdom of God in miniature. Sometimes when his mother could not understand the course which he was following, he would say to her that all he was doing was to take the love and the ideals which he had known within the limits of the family circle and to declare that henceforth in him they must be felt and applied without limit, to the ends of creation.

The life of the home centered in the Church. Bill's early life was full of it. And even into his twenty-fifth year it commanded his loyalty and devotion, and he poured into its service all that he then had in him.

He finished high school shortly before he was sixteen. Lafayette was the ancestral college of his family, and he went there as a matter of course. Here he came under the "heretical" influence of Professor John M. Mecklin, now at Dartmouth College, through whom he first learned not to be afraid to think, not to be afraid to place question-marks against tradition, and to undress the saints. He graduated in 1912 with Phi Beta Kappa standing and as valedictorian of his class.

In his last year, he had decided that he must become a minister, but his conclusions about Jesus made any orthodox seminary out of the question. His parents were strongly opposed to his going to so radical an institution as Union Theological Seminary, then the storm-center of heresy trials in the Protestant Church, and most would have yielded to parental pressure, but not Bill Simpson. He realized that no school could help him which did not meet his intellectual problems with a love for truth and an open-mindedness as fearless as his own. He knew that he would have to go to some seminary like Union or abandon the ministry altogether.

He was graduated in 1915 with a *magna cum laude*. Wishing for a hard task and one where he could be of the greatest possible service to his fellow men, and having at that time almost no knowledge of the problems that menaced the life of mankind in the world of economics, politics, and international relations, he had expected to go to India or China as a missionary. But during the summer of 1915 he was unexpectedly confronted with a momentous decision. He was called to be the assistant in a church of millionaires in a college town, which would certainly have been a stepping-stone to preferment in his profession. But he also had the opportunity of going to a broken-down church, in one of the most sordid industrial districts of New Jersey, which could make no definite promise of any salary whatever. He decided to take the latter, and there are those who think that all he has done since was contained in that choice.

~ 11 ~

It was while minister of this church that he took his stand against the War and also gradually moved toward socialism. So much so, that when the men of his church went to the heads of the factories to solicit contributions toward the larger church building which had come to be needed, the reply was, "Get that man Simpson out of here and you can have all the money you want, but not a cent so long as you keep him." Indeed, it gradually became evident that his radical protest against war on the one hand and against the iniquities of the economic order on the other was more than even most of his own church members could stand. Many of them withdrew, some who had been his staunchest supporters became his bitterest enemies. Agents of the Department of Justice came to listen to his sermons and stayed to warn him to stop such preaching, and to threaten him with imprisonment or secret abduction if he kept on. But he did keep on, until in the fall of 1918, feeling that the church was not his and that he had no right to break it up any further, he resigned. But in the resignation which he read both to his church people and to his presbytery, he declared that the Church was a prostitute and a Judas – a prostitute because it kept alive its body by selling its soul to those who secured power and money by the enslavement of men and women and children, and a Judas because it had betrayed Christ in going to war. And then gradually during the next two years he came to the conclusion that too many of the things which as a minister he had to believe and to do were in conflict with his deepest intuitions and convictions, that he could not be an honest man and be a minister at all. And so at last, in order to bring his life into conformity with his highest ideals, he went to the pains of getting unfrocked. If men ever listened to him again, he desired that it should not be on account of any human ordination, not because someone had laid hands on him and pronounced him a "reverend," but because they could not escape the truth and the beauty which were in what he said.

From the time when he left the Church to the spring of 1919 he was associate director of the National Civil Liberties Bureau, now termed the American Civil Liberties Union. But the real significance of these months lies in the fact that it was then he read for the first time the life of St. Francis of Assisi. This came as the greatest challenge he had known up to this time. Here at last was a man who was not forever singing and praying and talking about love, but who really loved, deeply, widely, everything on earth, and to that love gave all that he had. For the sake of that love he literally stripped himself, as he believed Jesus before him had stripped himself, and like him became a penniless beggar, without family, home, or possessions. All this affected Bill Simpson like wine. For days he was drunk with it. The love of these men! And the deeds that came from them – their courage, their abandon, and the literal correspondence there was between what they saw and what they said, between what they said and what the did, till their very lives took on the light and the color of their vision! Bill Simpson never got away from it. Being the kind of man he was, it was probably inevitable that in the end he also should have to strip himself for love's sake. But he was not ready to do it then. He was not equal to it. It was too sudden. It was too much. Moreover, he must take time to make very sure.

While making sure he decided to try out an idea which he had been turning over in his mind for some time. He was convinced that the capitalist system was a thing of stupidity and iniquity, and, though he did not believe in violence, he had thought that perhaps he might become a revolutionary organizer or agitator. In this connection he had wanted to find out first hand what men had to do in this country in order to make a living. So he resigned his position, and went to work with his hands. He picked coal in a breaker, and loaded it into cars down in a coal mine. He trimmed ore-cars in an iron mine, and narrowly escaped death from a fall of rock half a mile down in a copper mine. He made tires in Akron, operated a drill-press in Ford's factory in Detroit, bunked in a box car while he sweated with pick and shovel in a railroad section-gang in the Rockies, worked in a department store in Chicago and was kept awake killing bed-bugs in one of that city's fifteen-cent beds. During these months he came close to men of all sorts – trade unionists, socialists, I.W.W.'s. Of them all he admired most those who were most radical. And when he returned it was with his convictions about the capitalist system unaltered. But he returned with a new conviction – a profound conviction that even more than we needed a change of economic or political system, though this was needed desperately, we needed a new kind of man on this earth. And all the while – even in the dark depths of the mines – he had not been able to get away from St. Francis' vision of what that new man might be. But still he was not ready.

So he accepted a job teaching in the Brookwood School, later to become the first resident labor college in America, but then only a radically idealistic, free lance, progressive school. His major course perhaps typifies his thinking at this time. It was entitled "Our Economic System and Its Challenge to Christianity." But this year of teaching also was to prove for Bill Simpson a road which led nowhere. He had explored the Church as a field of Christian service, and had found it wanting. He had gone into the labor movement, only to find that it, too, needed changed lives as much as, or more than, a change in economic system. He was now to discover that this very idealistic school in which he was teaching, and which gave him his living, was supported on unearthed coal and steel dividends,* which for him then was blood money. He felt that to remain in the school would involve violation of some of his highest ideals. And so, in spite of his love for many of his comrades in the school, and in spite of the urgent invitation to become its head, at the end of the year he resigned.

With this door also closed against him he found himself confronted squarely with the necessity of deciding what he was going to do about the new vision of life which had come to him through St. Francis, and Tolstoy, and Jesus. He realized at last that he could put it from him no longer, that it alone called forth the highest that was in him, that whether or not he could find any other to go with him, he must go. And so in the fall of 1920, after a month of solitude on an island in the St. Lawrence River, he returned home to give away everything that he possessed, his money, his clothes, his furniture, his books.

* This has no reference whatever to the sources of income of the present Brookwood Labor College

All he kept for himself was a single suit of clothes and his carpenter's tools. And then he went to live in a foreign working-class quarter and made a gift of his labor, depending for his needs on what people wanted freely to give him.

After a time he began to speak on the streets (and often got arrested for it), and to young people in the city parks, or in churches, or in colleges. Many of the respectable people and the city authorities thought him unbalanced, but the students flocked to hear him, so that there came to be a small group living together in a little shanty, each man having a room to himself six feet square, with a board bunk for a bed, a wide shelf for a desk, and a store-box for a chair. The shanty they built themselves with materials given them by friends. They worked for people in the neighborhood, doing any kind of work they knew how to do. Sometimes they did carpentering or painting, sometimes they cut hair or sharpened knives, sometimes they dug ditches or chopped wood or scrubbed floors. They had a common purse, but usually there was very little in it. Sometimes it was quite empty. Sometimes they had to pick their coal from the ashes in the near-by city dump.

This was the kind of life to which Bill Simpson had been led by his uncompromising loyalty to truth as he saw it and by his unconquerable determination to follow the way of greatest love. One may disagree with much that he was doing at this time, but one must recognize that it was what seemed truest to his inner light and that he was absolutely fearless and uncompromising in his fidelity to it, cost what it might. For nine years he followed this austere way. Many college students were profoundly affected.

Even a millionaire's son gave up all his possessions to share the life of Bill Simpson.

But in 1927 it became evident that there was something wrong with his usually superb health. He seemed to require some kind of relaxation and change. Whereupon a large number of his friends, recognizing the situation and learning of the desire he had long felt to meet Gandhi, raised a fund to make it possible for him to go to India.

From the time he left San Francisco until he reached New York again he was never once in a hotel. In every country he visited he lived in native homes, and wherever he went he loved the people, whether they were Japanese, Chinese, Indian, or English. His experiences were many and varied. Once he traveled steerage lying in a crowded hold with a Japanese touching him on each side, and foot and head. He rolled on the floor with Kagawa's little boy. He stayed at Itto-en ("House-of-One-Light") on the edge of Kyoto, where a group of people, practicing Franciscan poverty but not celibacy, were gathered around Tenko Nishida, whose saintly life epitomizes and enshrines much of the highest wisdom of the East. With him Bill had very frank searching all-day talks which practically settled his long-growing conviction that the rejection of sex with which he had begun his venture of faith seven years before was wholly unsound. He was picked up on the streets of Singapore by a Mahomedan who was on his way to a large banquet being given to a notable Muslim missionary from India, and in the end found himself seated at the head table right beside the guest of honor. Attired in shorts, Gandhi hand-woven shirt and barefoot sandals, he marched and danced one night in the streets of Calcutta in an anniversary celebration of the Brahmo Samaj. He had a long talk with the poet Tagore, and for four days sat at the feet of Kshiti Mohan Sen, one of those great souls who sometimes hide themselves in a mantle of obscurity, who opened to him the treasures of Kabir and the songs of the other Sufi-like mystics who succeeded him, as probably no one else in the world could have done. Contact with this man, whose spirit is all light, helped to precipitate in Bill a spiritual crisis the exaltation of which brought him to a heightened and deepened realization of that which, more than her rivers or mountains, more than her temples or great men, India is – the realization that every man's *guru* is within himself. And this realization not only freed him from the need to see Gandhi, he even felt commanded not to go to meet him, to remember rather and always that his *guru* (or, if you prefer, his God) and the answer to all his problems were within himself. This conviction impelled him to cancel all his arrangements with Gandhi and return to America and go on with his work. And this, accordingly, after taking four days to make sure, he finally did, his soul singing the while, "Thy *guru* is within thee," and his spirit dancing in joy to the music of it. And in making this decision he always has felt that he did right.

After a short period for rest following his return from his trip (for physically it had proved rather a drain upon him), he went back to his little shanty located in a foreign quarter on the edge of Passaic for the final period of his life as a Franciscan. But within a year a son was born to him, and as this introduces a side of his experience which it would not have been easy to weave into the main theme of our story, it seems best to pause here while we bring this part of our narrative up to date.

The Franciscan sort of life to which Bill Simpson had dedicated himself had seemed to preclude any family responsibilities. And so, in spite of the fact that he was then in love with a girl who was as strong and idealistic in her way as he was in his, set celibacy before himself as his ideal. And yet, after two years, they married. How this came about he himself has recounted in his autobiographical pamphlet entitled *A Spiritual Quest and Venture of Faith,* concerning which John Haynes Holmes said, in publishing it, "We do not recall anything to compare with it in sheer sincerity and elevation of spirit since Tolstoy's personal writings on the subject." But in setting out together they pledged one another, in private and in public, that each must always be free to follow his highest light, even though in time it took them apart. After a year his wife, recognizing that she was not naturally Franciscan, withdrew to set up independently her little place in the hills of north Jersey, which Bill dreamed over with her and which, with his labor and his skill as carpenter and cabinet-maker, they transformed into the lovely place it became — for years the trysting-place of their closest friends and comrades. But even in these years their unity was deepest at those hours of common dedication in which they recognized that the highest they knew pointed them in ways that were different. They were nearest when outwardly they were apart.

By 1925 or 1926, largely under the influence of Carpenter and Whitman, Bill was coming to have grave doubts about the soundness of making celibacy an ideal.

To do this was to stigmatize sex as evil, and really to despair of one of the most fundamental parts of human experience. His meeting Tenko Nishida of Tokyo, in 1927, on his way to India, to which we have already alluded, helped to settle his belief, which has only grown stronger since, in the essential sanctity of sex.

In consequence, some time after his return a son was born. In him both father and mother have ever recognized the lovely symbol of their closest unity.

There was no understanding beforehand as to how the child should be supported. Both were sure that it was right he should come, and seem to have trusted, simply, that the further steps would become clear as the time for taking them drew near.

And perhaps they did thus become clear, but probably they were not steps that were anticipated by either of them. For months before the baby came, and for months after, Bill left his work and stayed with his wife. During the entire first year or two he came finally, after one of the most costly struggles of his life, to the settled certainty that in the particular situation in which he found himself, to take the part of a husband and a father in the full and ordinary sense was quite incompatible with his chief work in life. Torn so long, as he had been, between two very strong pulls, the domestic and the creative, the personal and the social, he saw at last that he must again put his mission singly first, regardless of consequences, or – go to pieces. He must stake everything quite simply on the faith that even to his wife and son his chief gift was himself, his life; that apart from his integrity he was, and could be, nothing, even to them. . . . Since 1931 he and his wife have lived apart, and they have been virtually separated. And during this time, throughout which he has had to be almost wholly absorbed in working out a new orientation to life, he left support almost entirely to his wife.

Father and son see one another whenever circumstances permit. They were together three months during the summer of 1934 on the farm which Bill now has in the Catskill Mountains. To the little lad his father is "Dadda," or often "Bill." A friend who saw them together writes, "Between these two there is a rare camaraderie. It is evident every hour of the day how close they are to one another. Often, at the end of the evening meal, the little fellow would say, 'Dadda, I want to sit on you.' And Bill would tenderly fold him in his arms, pillowing the sleepy head on his chest. So they would have quiet communion for a little while before the boy was tucked into bed."

At the present time Bill and his wife are cooperating in the care of the child. One feels that this experience has not yet come to a conclusion and that the final chapter about it cannot yet be written.

But now we must again pick up the main thread of our narrative.

Shortly after his return from India he went back to his shanty is Passaic to begin what was to prove to be his last effort, a very desperate one, to carry through the Franciscan sort of life on which he had set out eight years previously. But now all sorts of questionings and doubts began to press in upon him. He began to feel that the coat he had been trying to wear was not his coat. Whether it was too big for him or what, it did not fit him. It might have been Jesus' coat, or St. Francis' coat, but it was not his. Also, be became sure that if another man is lying in the gutter, even if he is being compelled to lie there, one does not necessarily help him best by lying down beside him. And again, it kept coming to him, "These people do not have ears for what I have to say. I do not belong here." And at last he was too much shaken to carry on any longer, and found in the owner's withdrawal of the further use of the lots on which his shanty had been built the final reason for leaving Passaic. But in his own soul he knew that it was the end of a period in his life, that he would never again try to live as he had tried to live there, that in the great idealistic venture of his youth, into which he had poured everything he had in him, he was beaten.

The period which followed was probably the most critical in Bill Simpson's whole life thus far. He was exhausted and very much alone. He was in the worst of throes of finding and following faithfully his true path in relation to his wife and child. And just at this time when he most urgently needed inner certainty and strength, he was torn loose from all his old moorings. He found it necessary to question everything he had believed, even the ideals which had been dearest and the beliefs that had been surest. He could not stand the thought of mumbling old shibboleths in the face of disturbing facts, or of seeking peace, ostrich fashion, by burying his head and refusing to think. On the contrary, he was determined to find, if it existed, amid the shifting sands and seas of this universe some solid rock which nothing could overthrow. Only on such could he venture to build again. And out of all that he had believed and reached toward, whatever *could* be destroyed he believed he would be well-rid of. Therefore he fairly dipped himself into acid, and turned upon all his strongest positions the most murderous guns he could find

– turned them upon the existence of God, on a moral order in the universe, the validity of the mystical experience, the Franciscan ideal, the teaching of Jesus, the ethics of non-violence and non-resistance, the principles of democracy, and the whole social philosophy based on belief in the equality of men, and of men and women. He passed, as it were, into solution, and for years he did not know whether anything would ever again crystallize into definite ideals and convictions. He did not know whether he would ever again have a way of his own, and see clearly in what direction it led, or find the strength to follow it if he saw it.

During this period, from about the fall of 1929 to the spring of 1932, he knocked about from one place to another, earning his way as a carpenter, securing as much time as he could for study and thought. At length he began to feel the need to live in the presence of the sea, or of great mountains, that he might have their vast quiet strength to draw upon. He longed to live close to the earth, away from the madness of cities, and to grow his own food with his own hands. And it was at this time that a friend, knowing of his need, gave him a farm near Prattsville, New York, high up in the Catskill Mountains. From then until the fall of 1933 he spent most of his time on this farm, in quiet work in the open air, and with his books, in constant thought. (For years his study was chiefly of Nietzsche, whom he read exhaustively, and whose essential message he came to believe agreed with that of Thoreau, and Whitman, and Blake, and Jesus.) What this place in the mountains has meant to him, no one will ever know but Bill Simpson. What would have happened without it even he does not know. For underneath the quiet surface of the simple life he led, a very desperate struggle went on, a struggle that he might become alive again, and well and whole; a struggle to hold himself together until a new sun rose upon him. It was the time when all his vital forces reached their lowest ebb. There were days when he wished only that he might go to sleep and be spared any awakening. It was a long cold dark night. But at last there were signs that the sun was coming, at first faint and doubtful, but then more and more unmistakable, and finally the sun himself, pouring his light over the hills, bringing ever clearer vision, sure convalescence, and a new joy. Until in the fall of 1933, after two and a half years of silence, he knew that he must again go out and speak – and again as before chiefly to young people.

At first glance what he has to say now is different from what he said five or ten years ago. And yet, if one looks more deeply, one sees that it is not so different after all. Certainly, he himself feels that he has in no sense turned his back on the message of love which bulked so large in his talks in the past; he only understands better now what true love is, has brought it into a more complete coordination with his thinking, and has carried it further. Without being less idealistic, he is more of a realist. He sees what as men we are and have to contend with in actually becoming what we have it in us to be. Also he feels now that there is nothing which could conceivably happen to him or be taken away from him that need disturb his certainty or cut off his inner source of strength.

Bill Simpson is not a social worker – nor a social reformer, at least not in any ordinary sense. He is a seeker of truth, and one who would fain follow whithersoever it may lead, no matter at what cost. He wants to see a nobler, grander species of man on this earth, and calls on men to spend themselves utterly for the realization of this end. As the first step in this direction he himself undertakes simply to incarnate his own vision in his own life. And he challenges other men to do the same thing, to find out what it is they themselves *want most deeply,* the profoundest most unappeasable yearning of their beings, and to set that free. He wants to see them stand forth before the world their simple naked selves, no matter what the cost to themselves or to others – to be out and out what most deeply they are.

It will be remembered that the greatest spiritual leaders from Jesus on down through the centuries have been accused of madness. Some there are who always claim that the sincere prophet is beside himself. One can disagree violently with Bill Simpson. One can feel that he has been unfair to his wife and home. One can quarrel with his ineffectiveness. But after all is said and done, one has to admire his faithfulness to the truth as he sees it. And who is there to say that America does not need this challenge? In an era when men are beginning to realize that the peoples of the world have bowed down and worshipped at the shrine of things; when it is becoming evident that materialistic standards result in a social kleptomania; and when at last all can see that capitalistic values are vanishing like snow in a spring thaw; who is there to say that Bill Simpson's way of life does not have value for our time? When the son of a great religious leader in America, after listening to Bill Simpson, can say, "I have been more challenged by that man than by any other speaker I ever heard, even if I don't agree with him," it is a tribute which cannot be ignored.

The only values of life that are real, the only goals which are worth the cost of life itself are spiritual, not material. One cannot measure the value of a single life which is dedicated uncompromisingly, fearlessly, self-sacrificingly, to the highest truth which that individual is capable of apprehending. The philosophy of Bill Simpson as a whole is not mine. But I reverence a soul who is willing to risk his life in searching for truth, and who, as he finds it, so weaves it into the very fabric of his life, that he can say, in deed and in truth, "My life is my message."

In closing this brief sketch I cannot perhaps do better than to quote the words in which Bill Simpson himself had recently summarized his own philosophy:

"I care about life. What I care about most is that I may find it, and that finding it I may arouse other men to a sense of the life which is in them also. I care that they should dig down to what most deeply they are, that without shame or apology or explanation but with heads thrown back, they should accept this, and avow it, and rest in it, as our fathers were taught to rest in the 'will of God' – which, psychologically speaking, is the same thing. I care that they should dare to stand forth before their fellows their naked selves. And this is enough. What happens to the Church, or Christianity, or Christian morality, or to ideas about God, really does not matter to me. Should they prove not to be a help but a hindrance to strong noble living, let them be sloughed off. After all, they never have been more than means.

But the end is life – rich, true, strong, varied, exalted life –
on this earth."

JEROME DAVIS

Yale University Divinity School,
New Haven, Connecticut,
December, 1934.

I. *Yea to Life*

What I am about to say is not intended for everybody. I warn you: it is intended only for those who have ears for it. For others I would say something very different – possibly the direct opposite. And so, if you do not like what I say, if you find it uninteresting, or in part unintelligible, or offensive, or if, having heard my words, you are one who can forget them, then do not let yourself be overmuch disturbed by them. Do forget them. You are certainly not one of those to whom I am speaking. I am really speaking only to those who have ears for what I have to say – who have, as it seems to me, a rare kind of ear for a rare kind of music.

I care about life. My concern is not for mere human existence, not for keeping breath in every scrap of humanity that is still able to drag itself around. My concern is for quality of life and for ever grander quality. I care that there should be on this earth life that is rich, and beautiful, and strong, and exalted. But on every hand it seems to me that such life in men is being beaten. Life is to be found, of course, only in individuals, but on every hand the individual is being overwhelmed by the mass, and in the name of the mass. Everyone is being called upon to bend the knee to the great ox-god Baal, which is the human herd, and everywhere men have succumbed. They have become as alike as tin-cans and tooth-picks – and just about as significant. They are afraid to be different. In America to be different is the unforgivable sin. In every child that comes into the world it seems that life undiscouraged tries afresh, in the hope, as it were, that perhaps here at last my be one in whom it may come to complete fulfillment. But the child is hardly born before society on every side begins to crush down upon him with its pressure, until slowly the individual is tripped, trapped, caged, cowed, seduced, suffocated, or crushed, into submission.

Our whole social set-up does it. Our homes, our schools, our churches. On every side the child is greeted with "Thou shalt," "Thou shalt not." There is so little reverence before the life in the child; so little effort to help the young person find out what seems true to *him;* what to him is most worth living and dying for. Everywhere education is a matter of something stuck on from the outside, like so much paint and plaster. Also, in every government, whether it be a dictatorship or a democracy, we have the top-heavy centralized state crushing down upon the individual with its demands, and everywhere people are coming to believe that once the government has spoken there is no recourse left but to obey. In our industries, men by increasing millions are learning simply to take orders, to do as they are told, and are compelled, if they are to exist, to let this living thing which is their personality be subjected for the working hours of the day to a dead and utterly alien master – the factory machine. And more and more the syndicates of the press and the broadcasts of the radio are causing a large part of the people, not only of a nation but of a whole civilized world, to be hit at the same moment with the same ideas. All of which is resulting in uniformity. And wherever you have life becoming uniform, it is a sign that is has not been strong enough to take the shape and direction which belong to it. It has been beaten.

And our resistance to this overpowering influence of society has been to no small extent undermined by our very philosophy and religion. Christianity, as it has come down to us, has given us a herd ethics. The well-being of the mass is placed above the integrity of the individual. A thing called love, but which is even a denial of the highest love if it involve a betrayal of life, has been exalted above trueness. We have been exhorted to "render service," to "do good," and to "help others," even though it be at the price of turning our backs on that farthest, rarest, and most socially significant *life* in us, which is contained in our own highest vision. The individual is required to subordinate himself to the mass, whose demands press in upon him so hard that he is usually left with a sick conscience if he does not stand ready to set aside not only his job and his family but his deepest insights, his surest convictions, in order to become an effective instrument for the welfare of the greatest number. The well and the capable are given to believe that they have spent their years most worthily if they have spent them on the sick and the inferior. The strong are told it is their duty to load themselves down with the burdens of the weak. The tall are called upon in the name of love to stoop low and make themselves small that they may be heard by little people with deaf ears. The swift are asked to take pity and to accept the pace of the slow that they may be helpful to cripples. And the result is a frightful leveling of life, mediocrity of life, and denial of life. The result is that the life in people of exceptional possibilities is lost; they are prevented from making to the advancing life of mankind their *greatest* gift, which is their own true selves. And wherever an individual fails of his fulfillment there is a dead cell in the body of society.

And yet this is happening on every side, and it is happening in large part because men have so long been taught that it is more important to be loving than to be true. People today have almost no sense of what is in them. It is almost impossible to find anyone who knows what he really wants to do and who is doing it. Everywhere people are saying – not what they really believe, but what they have been taught they ought to believe. They are living at second-hand. They do, not what they themselves see but what somebody else says. Everywhere life is starched and collared. Everywhere men are dying without ever having really lived. In our so-called virtue especially, there is no leap, no spontaneity, no elemental force, no blood, no joy. In other words, life is everywhere tamed, weak, falsified, uniform, mediocre, "good"; that is, beaten – if not dead.

But I *care* about life. I care that there should be on this earth life that is rich, beautiful, strong, and exalted. I am looking for him who knows what it is to plumb deep-deep-deep down, until he comes to *that which he himself wants* – only, mark you, wants *most deeply;* and who will accept this, and avow it, and rest in it, as our fathers were taught to rest in the will of God; who, at last, with his head thrown back, without fear, without shame, without apology and without explanation, will stand forth before the world his simple naked self. I am looking for him who has got down to that most unappeasable yearning in his being; to that in him which is such that so long as everything else comes to him but this comes to him not, then everything that does come to him turns to dust in his hands and ashes in his mouth; to that life in him which is such that once he does find it and does yield himself to it utterly – then, though everything else is taken away from him, though he has to go cold and hungry and alone, though he knows no human being on this earth into whose eyes he can look and find understanding, though everything he has sweated bloody sweat for, men bring to what they call failure, and his very life they bring to what they call death, he shall yet be able to go his way softly singing in his heart. To do this is to live; and to fail to do this, no matter how good the reason for the failure may be, is to do what most men do – to die without ever having really lived at all.

II. *The Way to One's Spring*

But how does one find such life?

Well, I have to confess that in the last analysis I do not know. I really do not understand how life gets into a little child. Much less do I understand how it is that this kind of life comes to some men and not to others. And yet there are some things about it which I can say with the uttermost certainty. For one, this life is not far off. It is not up in the sky. It is not in a book. It is not in someone who lived a long while ago. It is nearer than our hands or our feet, nearer than our breathing. It is within our own selves. Did you ever take an acorn and with a knife lay it open? At its heart lies the kernel, a very little and seemingly insignificant thing. And yet there is in that kernel something wonderful, and fearful. For if it but get warmth and moisture, then will it begin to nose roots deep down into the hard earth. Yes, nose them down with such insistence that if it be caught in the cleft of a rock then will it fairly split that rock asunder. There is that in it which, with those conditions fulfilled, will unfold the trunk and the bark which belong to the oak tree, and take the form against the sky that belongs to the oak tree, with the buds all bunched at the ends of the twigs, and with each little bud having the exact number of scales that belongs to the oak tree. All locked up in an acorn! But if this is a thing of miracle and wonder, do you think that you and I, human beings, are any less creatures of miracle and wonder? Oh,

I tell you, every one of us at first has within him the nucleus of a life all his own – some as yet unspoiled sense of what he really likes, of what is good for him, of what he has it in him to be, and of the way he is meant to go – of his destiny. And all his potential powers are there for it to feed upon and select from, to be organized by it and knit into it, and by it shaped into a life different from any that ever has been. It is like the unfertilized cell in an egg. And there it sleeps, waiting somehow to be stabbed awake, to be impregnated. But if once that impregnation does take place, then it begins to reach out and out in an effort to gather into itself every power that we have in us – all the blood and brawn and brain of us; all our vision, and love and endurance; every passion and capacity we have – and to shape us into an organic whole, which is our own true life.

But if I can not know for a certainty that this kind of life will come to one man and not to another, still I do know that it will come only to him who wants it. Was it not said, "Blessed are they who hunger and thirst, for they shall be filled" and again, "Seek and ye shall find?" Only, to bring out fully the intensity which was behind those words, it seems that we should say rather, "Seek, and *seek,* and SEEK, and then ye shall find." But if we do not really care, why should we find? We certainly shall not, even if we think we should. But every man who seeks with desperateness cannot fail to find his way. He develops in himself a sense for life which is like unto a camel's sense for water. He smells it from afar and, once he has the sniff of it in his nostrils, nothing shall stop him.

But this germ of what we are does not merely lie there sleeping. It is constantly throwing out intimations of its presence to catch our attention. It is a god imprisoned in a dungeon who is ever trying to get secret messages through to us to let us know that he stands waiting for us to come and set him free. What do I mean? I mean, for instance, that when you are reading a book and something quick and instinctive rises up in recognition of the truth or beauty in the words before you, then you catch a glimpse of the truth and beauty buried deep within yourself, waiting to be set free. When you read Emerson's words, "Trust they self – every heart vibrates to that iron string," and you find your own heart vibrating to it; or read, "It makes one happier to love than to be loved," and find your own heart pulsing its confirmation; in that moment it is as though your own lit-up face stood forth from the darkness and you catch a glimpse of that which most deeply you are. Thus gradually you build up a knowledge of what your deepest life is like.

Or you come across some spiritual titan, either out of the past or in the world about you. You stand, let us say, in the presence of Thoreau, refusing to pay taxes to a state that supports slavery, and in consequence going to jail; or of Gandhi, stripping himself naked in order to deliver his people from a foreign yoke and from the even more degrading yoke of their own weakness; or before Nietzsche, all his life yearning for friends, having the powers which could have brought him fame and influence in his own day if only he had been willing to compromise with his vision, yet, for truth's sake, so sternly holding his course that he knows only loneliness, and obloquy, and poverty, and unspeakable pain and finally suffers complete mental collapse. And if, as you thus stand in the presence of this voluntary crucifixion of life for the sake of fuller life for mankind, a deep stillness settles over you and out of this stillness your soul cries "Would to God that I were like that!" then, the great secret is, that that is what you are like. That is what you really want; that is the god in you waiting to be set free.

Or some day through all its hours you have known a certain inner soreness, some dumb heaving, something within you that would fain be delivered. And you have a date for a dance for the evening. Yet you recognize at last that what you really want is simply to be alone, away from everything, and everybody, out on some hilltop, under the stars. And if you are obedient to the inner behest; if you have the sense and the courage to break the date and get alone on the hilltop under the stars, then miracles may happen. Have not all the seers said it! Then something may be spoken to you which you will never be able to forget. At such moments the scales fall from one's eyes and one sees things that make life forever after totally different. Something happens which is like a lightning-flash from a far horizon, lighting up the whole landscape, so that one sees clearly (though but for a moment) the road which is one's own road winding its way over the hills. Or it may be like a star surprising us from between clouds, a star of such beauty that once our eyes have beheld it, then thereafter, go where we may or do what we will, underneath all our going or doing we are only secretly waiting and hoping that that star may show itself from behind the clouds again; that seeing it, we may know it for the same star, and know it as our star, and fix our eyes upon it forever. Or in these moments it may be, perhaps more than anything else, as though we gazed deep into the eye of our one Beloved. And oh, this is the critical time. For if once we really behold him, if once we do look deep into the depths of his eyes, deep into the depths of what most deeply we are, then thereafter are we utterly damned. Then thereafter are we utterly lost to all ordinary ways of feeling, and thinking, and doing, lost to orthodoxy, and respectability, and virtue, and a career. For the drunkenness and witchery and folly of a strange new love have entered into us and possessed us, and whither he goes we go – forever. Thereafter we know that we belong together, and for better or for worse and as long as life shall last, whether men like it or not, we go together.

In this experience one stands closest to the core and the quick of one's life. Here one comes nearest to touching reality nakedly, and to knowing oneself in relation to it. You may call it God, or not – that does not matter. But here you have an exquisite sense of value by which you know intuitively what is light for you and what darkness; what food and what poison; what true and beautiful, strengthening, enlarging, and full of life, and what is false and ugly, fettering, narrowing, and deadening. Here is your central sun, illumining for you all that you look out upon, revealing it at its true worth; and around it your whole life is meant to swing. Here is your ballast, by which your ship can ride the fiercest tempest on an even keel, and your ever-present pocket-compass, which – if you can hold it still enough – will never fail to point your way out of every woods. Here is your Commander, whose will is your only law; and your Judge, whose verdict is your final authority. Aye, and here also is your one Beloved, whose mere averted eyes drive you worse than any judge, in utter unity with whom lies your life, and to whom at last you must give yourself, body, mind, and soul. He is always at your side, but he comes closest when you are stillest. His greatest secrets, his deepest wisdom, his tenderest love he shares with you only when the voice of every other impulse is so stilled that you can hear him in a whisper. He is not "God," but he *is your* God – your Law, your very Life, your very Self; and into his touch upon you is distilled the knowledge of all that you really want, and of all, in any actual situation, that you really need.

But if the first part of finding our deepest life is a matter of becoming sensitive to its presence, the second part is in obeying its behests. In all the universe there is no more inexorable law than this: use your eyes or lose them. Struggle with every power that is in you to live up to all your highest vision of truth and beauty, or begin to go blind. *Do* what you see, or yield yourself to what is no less than a creeping leprosy of soul, a deadness which will begin to crawl over – not your body, but over the very soul of you, over the only thing in you which is sensitive to truth and beauty, and which alone can give life on this earth any meaning; until at last you are unable to tell the difference between light and night. You have won a prize examination by cheating and your life tells you to go and confess it. Do you do it, or don't you do it? You can't believe the Creed. Do you keep on saying it, or don't you? You don't believe in the war. When the screws are applied, do you refuse to go or do you allow your fears and the need of your family and all sorts of rationalization to furnish you with justification for what is called "making an adjustment?" Yes, there is that in you which hungers so remorselessly for utter sincerity that your soul balks at so much as saying that you are glad to see a man who comes to your door when as a matter of fact you are sorry. But in all of these things, *do* you make your outside match your inside? *Are* you relentlessly honest, true to all the life that is in you? Or do you let yourself slip into the fatal habit of playing fast and loose with your light? Following it or not following it according to whether or not it is safe, comfortable, expedient or effective to do so? Right here it is decided whether a man goes on to ever fuller life or whether he begins to become more and more dead. If, having vision, he follows it not, then like the moles born into the caverns of Luray, with eyes which they do not use, gradually he goes blind. Expect to step off a cliff without falling, expect to handle molten iron without getting burned, expect to be struck by a bolt of lightning without being killed, but do not think that you can trifle with your light without having the very optic nerve of your soul gradually go dead.

Yet if that is true and to be heeded as a warning against disobedience to one's vision, the glad reverse is true – no less. We are born into labyrinths, confusing complexes of criss-cross passage-ways choked with darkness, and sometimes we utterly despair of ever finding our way out into the light. And yet, for each of us, leading right from where he now stands, there runs a golden luminous cord, winding its way down through the dark. And if he will but keep that cord in his hands, rolling it into a ball as he goes, he shall not fail to come out at last into the full sunlight and the great open places where the free winds blow. I mean to say, if a man but begin some day, wherever he is, to be absolutely true to all the light that is in him, living up to whatever measure of comprehension of truth he has, be it never so little; then, as in Jesus' parable of the talents, because he has made us of what he had, his vision shall increase and increase. Yea, that man shall be like one who arose from his bed while yet it was night, and went out into the open, and set his face toward the first faint flushes of light in the east, and held it there. Every minute the sun shall rise upon him higher; every hour the way he must go shall stand forth more clearly in its rays; until at last he shall walk with his whole being flooded in the light of it. All because what he *saw,* he *said;* that which to the bottom of him he *believed,* he *did.*

III. *Obstacles and Seductions*

But if any man does set it squarely before him to go straight through with the highest light that is in him, then bit by bit a way which is his own way begins to limn forth out of the darkness. It will be a way which, whatever its outer resemblance to the ways of other men, will really be original and unique. But as soon as a man steps off the beaten track there are all sorts of obstacles within him and without him over which he is apt to trip. And on every side there are sirens which would seduce him from his path. I should like to bring to your attention some of these which seem the most important.

Perhaps the one on which most people first become snagged is the love of security and the lust of possessions. I submit to you: Do not most of us think first about what we shall eat and what we shall drink and wherewithal we shall be clothed? And are not most of us ready to turn aside from faithfulness to our ideals for the sake of that which money can buy – for nice clothes with which to satisfy our vanity and maintain our social position; for the comfort and security of home and servants; for an automobile or the power over our fellows which comes to him who has money in abundance? No matter what we say, would it not seem that we really think to ourselves: first I must get a job and keep a job, and get most of the other things which I want, and then, into what space if left, I will crowd the living of my ideals?

Now I do not mean to say that all of these things are of no consequence. I know perfectly well that no man can get far on an empty stomach. But I know now on the basis of experience what once I had to take only on insight and faith – that he who does put first things singly first shall find that all the things which he needs, or even all the things needed by those dependent upon him, will somehow gravitate to him.

Or again, it is a question of what kind of life one wants. One day it dawned upon me that life upon this earth for most of us is like life in a little village with a dazzling mountain peak towering behind it. Look at this little village! So shut in by the wall all around it that its life is confined and has no outlook! People so closely herded together that everyone has to breathe another's breath and that they are all grown shamefully dependent and as timid as rabbits! Life here so narrow, flat, stuffy, safe, and commonplace! And into this village I was born, as we all are born. But one day I lifted my eyes and discovered the mountain rising above me. And looking closely, I saw the figures of men toiling across its yawning crevasses, with bleeding hands and feet scaling its dizzy cliffs, blazing trails and cutting toe-holds in the rock for those who would come after, and from all sides approaching its dazzling snow-covered summit. Yes, your Christ, and Blake and Whitman, and Nietzsche and Vivekananda, and others of the same dauntless succession! And once I had discovered these men up there on the heights, then thereafter life in this little village, so safe and stuffy, became insufferable. I also had to try to climb after them. And once a man even from the lowest slopes of the mountain has sniffed the air so crisp and clean, which no man has breathed before him, has caught the grand outlook, range after range of mountains stretching out before him, and has known the comradeship of even a few others who also see and dare and do; oh, after that, how can he any more go back to the stuffiness of the village, and the confinement of life on the flats, or to the cheap chit-chat of ordinary human intercourse?

But you cannot scale dizzy cliffs in a full dress suit and a high hat! You cannot fly on outspread wings in the face of the sun with your pockets weighted with gold and a mansion strapped to your back! If you also would go where those others have gone, you must strip yourself light, even as they did. Yes, it is costly. All I can say is that if the cost were ten times what it is, it would be worth it. And to him who stands torn both ways, looking one minute at the figures of those struggling far up the side of the mountain and then back again to the warmth and security of the village, to his soul standing thus in crisis and at its hour of decision, my soul cries, "What man *is* is more than anything he can possess. Would you not rather say out the thing that is in you though you died for it the next minute, than fill out seventy years, dragging through every one of them some secret sense that the thing you saw you never quite dared say, that the thing you most wanted to do and believed most worth doing you never quite had the abandon to do? What ever shall make up to a man for the haunting suspicion that he is a coward and a liar, that he has really sold himself and betrayed his fellow men for the sake of security and position? What shall it profit a man to gain all these things, and never really live? I say to you, Beware, lest by your fear of insecurity you be blinded and bewitched, and by your very possessions you come to be possessed, until these things you think you want (but are not at all what you want most?) become hobbles around your ankles and a noose around your neck. I cry with Nietzsche, Choose a life which is a bit dangerous. 'Blessed be moderate poverty.'"

If love of security and lust for possessions be the obstacle over which the majority of people trip first, that which brings down most of those who rise above economic concerns, is their love for those who are nearest and dearest to them. Jesus said, "a man's foes shall be they of his own household." Often they are his worst foes, and it was not without reason that he uttered those terrible words about family loyalties which I consider the severest words on this matter that have ever passed the lips of man. The evidence would seem to support the statement of C.G. Jung, the eminent modern psychologist,* that "Jesus' teaching separates man from his family without consideration." And sometimes I have felt, as I have seen how men succumb to their loved ones, that we should again have to enjoin upon young men that, at least during the period when they are passing through the throes of finding themselves, they break off all relations with their fathers and mothers.

Now do not misunderstand me. I see the parents' side also, and I know from experience how exalted the spirit of parents can be, and how much they have to give. And if it were always so, there would be no difficulty. For the love of such parents imposes no obligation in return.

* Psychology of the Unconscious, p. 454.

The thought and labor given to the child are not bestowed calculatingly as an investment to be paid back with interest out of the very life of the child in the days of one's own declining strength and lonely old age. Here as always love simply gives, and in the giving itself finds its sufficient satisfaction. It always leaves free.

Not that such a parent will never cross his child, especially in its youngest years – though even there, as little as possible. But from the day of its birth, he will look upon it not as wax to be impressed with his own image or molded after some other pattern of his own choosing, but always as a seed which is meant to unfold according to a bent and a necessity that are within itself. He sees his part in furthering that unfolding and in helping to bring it to fulfillment. However much he may lay within reach of his child the very richest and soundest of the heritage of the race which he himself knows, yet, he will always leave the child free to accept or reject. He keeps a certain distance. He has reverence before his child. He sees his high privilege in being the one to whom the child will first turn for help in his struggle for sure self-knowledge. And he feels that in the achievement of that knowledge and in the living faithfulness to the bent and direction which that knowledge reveals lies the fullest and possible return for all that he ever did for the child. It has been for this that he has prayed since the moment the child began to form in its mother's womb.

But most parents are not so. At birth they greet us with smiles, but before ever we have learned to walk they tightly bind our unformed feet with their "Thou shalts" and their "Thou shalt not's." With the result that by the time we find out what has been done to us – if we ever find out – it is too late: we never learn to run – hardly even to walk. We remain crippled for life. Or again, all the efforts of parents to foist upon their children the ambitions and ideals which they were unable to realize themselves, and to find in their children's achievements a compensation for their own failures – what is it all but narrow egotism? Or, yet again, the way they try to hold their children to themselves and for themselves by constantly instilling the duty to love them, the duty to honor and obey them, the duty to support them – where is there any love in this? What does it all come to but possessiveness and self-seeking? I tell you, in all this – and I am afraid it is the prevailing attitude of parents – there is not a thing for the life of a child that has reached the age of responsible choice. For a brief while the very selfishness of the parents may have helped to make a nest in which the tender life could take form, but now it has become the unyielding shell which the chick must somehow break if ever it is to step out into a larger life. Now it has become the flower-pot by which the roots of the potential oak are bound, and whose close hold it must somehow throw off if it is not to die. And yet see how every effort of the young life to find some crack in its prison-wall through which it can nose its way out and down into larger deeper life is almost always successfully turned. It is turned by the parents' appeal to the child's love; turned by his fear to trust himself in the face of his parents' practical pessimism, their "Many have tried it before you, and all have failed. It can't be done"; turned by the psychological astuteness and dialectical cleverness in the toils of which they get their immature and inexperienced child so tangled and confused that he is seized with panic and breaks down; turned by a haunting sense of guilt long ago instilled by his parents for all breaches of filial piety, and by the fear of a God invoked to punish those who do not follow the ways laid down by their elders.

In the face of all this I stand up and say NO! Out of such parents it is only weakness that speaks. In them life has been beaten. And where their children are being broken by their smallness and poisoned by their defeats, I would have no mercy on them. I would not have life sacrificed to their weakness, their smallness, their selfishness. I would urge a young person to have understanding for his parents, and to be patient and gentle if he possibly can, but in any case I would urge him to be as immovable as mountains are immovable and as inexorable as the stars in their courses.

Now again, do not misunderstand me. Not for a minute am I saying that every man should leave his father and mother. Really, as I warned you at the outset, I am talking only to him who knows what it is to have a life of his own. I am only saying again, "First things first." I am saying that whenever the conflict does come, the conflict which I believe must come to this sort of man sooner or later, between loyalty on the one hand to family and closest friends, and loyalty on the other hand to all he calls God, then let him beware lest his love for those who are dearest to him seduce him into infidelity.

I know it is hard to suffer, and that for a sensitive heart it is ever the worst of suffering to cause suffering to others. I know that before the prospect of taking a step which may break your parents' hopes and dreams, the will in you fairly turns to liquid and you cry out, "I cannot. I simply can not." But it is precisely here that I would take my place by your side and say to you quietly, "You must. For their sake as much as for your own, you must. I value gentleness and harmony in human relationships, but I value trueness more. I know that there can be no real harmony based on lies. All my experience, and it is a long and most searching one, has convinced me that trueness is the truest love – in the long run. Do not fear suffering – not even causing it to others. Do not let your deepest life languish in a flower-pot. Do not succumb to the close hug of your father and mother's hold upon you. Break it – as gently as you can, but break it. If necessary, break even them – as perhaps Jesus broke his mother Mary. First things first!"

Most of what I have been saying has very close bearing on the relations of men and women also. Indeed, in the case of men, they usually stand in less danger in their relations with their parents than with their wives and children. Rodin has the whole thing in his piece of sculpture entitled "The Eternal Idol," where a woman on her knees but leaning backward, with body thrust forward but arms hanging loose, receives between her breasts the bearded face of a man who kneels before her in servile longing for her embrace: most men are caught between the legs of some woman, and lie prostrate before the sex in her. There is hardly one man in a thousand who will not put aside his ideals, his highest vision, everything which for him is God, in order to get the girl he loves or to be able to stay with the girl he has married. Moreover, there are all the ways which the wiles of woman have with a man. Nietzsche said, "Women always intrigue privately against the higher souls of their husbands," and as a generalization his statement is true. And such *must most* women be. For, again speaking generally, the instinct in man is to create, and the instinct in woman is to procreate. She is more physical than man, lives closer to the earth, and, naturally and justly since to her is committed the continuation of the race, once she is with child she is almost certain to be overwhelmed with a veritable tidal wave of sheer biological concern for security. And a reasonable degree of security both she and the child ought to have. And if you as would-be creator feel that you cannot do your work and provide that security, then you had better simply refrain from marrying. Which does not mean at all that I am advocating celibacy. As a matter of fact, for celibacy as an ideal, for celibacy which grows out of a sense that sex is evil, for that kind of celibacy, in spite of the fact that it was once my own position, I have neither use nor respect. And indeed, a great deal is to be said against celibacy on almost any grounds. The suppression of the sex instinct is commonly attended with a great many deep, and subtle, and far-reaching disturbances and perversions in a person's whole psychological make-up. Also, I think it an extremely exceptional person who can reach his or her completest fulfillment or make his or her greatest gift to the world, without finding that other one who is the counterpart of his or her own soul. I believe, therefore, that a marriage which grows out of the realization of a deep unity between a man and a woman is very much to be desired, and should be forsworn only by one who is sure of himself and who knows the gravity of what he is undertaking.

What I am saying is this: let him who has extreme ideals by which he is resolved to live no matter whither they may take him, who feels in himself the power to create, who, whatever his form of expression, feels that at heart he is an artist, let him make terribly sure of the girl. Let him have nothing to do with a girl who does not love him most of all for his vision, and whose dedication to it is not as utter as his own. Let her be a girl who so fully shares his purpose that he would stake his very life on her certainty to say to him at the first and every crisis that might menace his loyalty to his vision, "You must never turn aside from your path for the sake of security for me, or even for the sake of security for our children. Your first responsibility is to that universal human family to which we also belong. Your chief gift to us as to mankind if your own true self. Without your integrity you are worth nothing to anybody, not even to me. The chief meaning of my presence by your side is to enable you to go farther than would be possible to you without me. To this high end I have dedicated myself. And for this we will risk everything in the faith that all we need will come to us. What does not come thus, we will go without." If a woman does not have the spirit to talk to you so, keep away from her. Keep away from her as from the devil and as from your destroyer. For if she overpowers your resistance and you marry her, you will discover at last that you have married your enemy, that you have taken under your armor one who slowly presses a dagger into your heart, and that the closer you press her to you the deeper you press that dagger toward your death.

Or if it be the case of husband and wife whose life together began in the deepest unity but who have come to the mutual recognition that the unity they had is gone, and that all their long patient prayerful efforts to revive it have failed completely, then I would say to them, "Better that you go your separate ways. Long enough have we had these three-legged races, in which neither man nor woman joyously runs but both only hobble. Unity is a blessed thing, but it is not a thing that can be preserved by pretense, or restored by trying to act after it is gone as if it still existed. And for a man and a woman capable of a deep unity to live together without it as husband and wife is a profanation. It is an adultery that blasts the soul. It is better for the man, better for the woman, better for the child, better for all those in the world whom their lives may touch, that each should walk — yes, in the deepest possible love for one another — but yet, with a love for their uttermost vision which is beyond all other loves. Beware, lest any lesser love seduce you into infidelity of soul."

The significance of what I have been saying about the relations of men and women may be summed up in a few words. The creative must not be swallowed up in the procreative. Mankind must not merely go on, but go ever higher. The arrow which indicates the direction of his life must point not to the horizon but to the stars. Because the reproductive is stronger in woman than in man, it must fall to man especially to see that the creative masters the procreative, whether in woman or in himself, and that the procreative is made to serve the creative. He must hold both himself and her to the demands made upon them by the loftiest goals the race has set before itself, so that procreation may be upon ever higher levels. The man, therefore, must be so sure in himself that the woman can rest in him; and he must be strong enough and noble enough for her to feel that he is worthy of the headship and the leadership, the love and the surrender of herself, which it is her very instinct, and desire, and fulfillment to yield to him.

The next siren against which I feel it important to warn you is – Christian morality. Perhaps I had better call it Christian pity. Here is a man, let us say, before whose eyes has arisen the star which at last he knows to be his star, and who is struggling with all that is in him to follow it faithfully. Only to discover, perhaps, that it takes him a way which is very extreme, very different from the ordinary ways. And as he struggles along, upon every side men cry to him – the hungry, the cold, the blind, the broken, and those grown dumb beneath oppression – and the natural humanness of his heart responds to the piteous cry of their need. And so long has it been dinned into his ears that his first duty is to "do good," to "help others," and to "render service," that he feels branded with the odium of "selfishness" if he persists in following his star and does not stand ready to turn aside from it in order to put salve on sores and to make himself a crutch for the beaten and broken. He is stricken with a sick conscience and feels positively guilty, before mankind, before his God, before the gaze of his own soul. So that in the end, in the vast majority of cases, he finally breaks down under the burden of his own integrity: he turns aside; and he who was sent to give men a life – his own simple self, with whatever meaning for the life of other men this might have, even as Jesus did – instead, forsakes his own course merely to alleviate suffering and to ameliorate conditions. And therein he is like a man to whom was entrusted oil to keep a light burning in a lighthouse that ships at sea caught in a storm might know where they were and kept off the rocks. But living in the village at the foot of the lighthouse there were people of his own kin overtaken by famine, and they pleaded with him piteously to give them of his oil, that they and their children might live and not die, and their children's children bless him forever. Until finally he yielded to their entreaties and gave to satisfy the pangs of their hunger the oil which was meant to keep the lighthouse burning. And the light went out, and ships at sea, caught in a storm, lost their way and perished on the rocks.

When a man thus plays Judas to his own soul, he both turns his back on his own highest potentialities and betrays the advance of mankind toward its noblest ends. I would like to see such a man take a good dose of sand and grit, to stiffen his spiritual backbone. I would like to see him put himself through a process of hardening so that he could hold a cutting edge and keep a rapier point – even when that edge and point cut and pierce the hearts of those he loves most. I would cry to him, "Do not be so pitiably accommodating! Don't be so ready to take any part that conventional requirements may press upon you, and to squeeze your life into any cranny that church morality may declare 'loving,' 'unselfish,' and 'Christ-like.' Have a shape and a size, a color and a direction that belong only to you; have some identity of your own, and in the steadfastness of your fidelity to it be as unalterable as the tides of the sea.

Now I am not saying that there is *no* place for pity. Pity is one of the herd-virtues, and all those who do not know what it is to have a life of their own to live, who have

~ 55 ~

no sense of what I mean by having a star to follow, all such people belong to the herd and the herd-virtues are the only ones that really fit them and that could make them happy. Those who do not have a life of their own to live, must *make* a life for themselves out of serving the life of others. They will reach their highest sense of fulfillment, their deepest satisfaction, precisely when they most completely efface themselves and with greatest abandon sacrifice themselves to the life of others. Their supreme virtue is "doing good." They find their true place as moral bell-hops and water-boys, as spiritual nursemaids.

Nor am I really saying anything against helpfulness in itself. I am only saying, Let your help to others be what you yourself really are, the impact on their life of your own integrity. Let your help be such as you can give while you pursue the course which belongs to you, but do not forsake that path to help anyone. Be like Gandhi, who, at one crisis in the struggle he was waging for his people in South Africa, left his wife, as they both thought, on her death-bed, to go and serve his cause. Be like Jesus, who, in order that he might "see of the travail of his soul and be satisfied," or, if you prefer, in order that he might follow his destiny to its very end, chose and held to a course which destroyed the unity of his family and broke his mother's heart.

"But this sounds to me like nothing but a plea for the rankest selfishness!" perhaps you exclaim. Ah! There you have it! Have I not just said it? It is with that judgment that the smug herd whips the individual, and especially the most loving and sensitive individual, back into line. Under the incubus of that little two-syllabled word "selfish" it ignorantly crushes the idealist's creative aspiration into submission and insignificance.

I say "ignorantly," for they seem not to know that it is impossible for any living creature to do anything whatever except for the sake of some satisfaction for itself. This is the very principle of life. To lose it would leave one as helpless in the face of this universe as an animal that had lost its instincts: one would never know surely which way to go, and would often like what was injurious. If to keep the instinct for one's own life be "selfish," then all men are selfish. For all men alike seek that which they believe will mean some increase in their own life, and if they are not to perish they *must* seek it. This is no more true of the social butterfly or the rapacious capitalist or the drunkard in the gutter than it was of Jesus of Nazareth. Was it not said of the expected Messiah, "He shall see of the travail of his soul and be *satisfied?*" The only difference is in the degree of wisdom that inspires the desires. The only difference is in the quality of the satisfactions, and in the plane on which they are sought. But here the difference may indeed be vast. For, on the one hand, the satisfaction one desires may be mere bodily excitation, which one is willing to seek even though it blights one's own higher powers and drags down one's dependents into a sea of misery and degradation. Or, on the other hand, one may so completely have identified one's own good with the highest good of mankind that one stands ready for its sake to be fairly blotted out of existence and in this voluntary self-immolation would reach the deepest joy of all. Yet – forget it not – even the martyr goes his way in quest of some increase in his own life. It has been said that Jesus died to save the world. I say that he died fully as much to save himself. Having said what he had said, up and down the land, having himself created the issue which menaced his very existence, to have turned back or to have turned aside would have been to have died a death far more fearful than that which he did die. Never again would he have been able to face himself. To move onward, to "set his face steadfastly to go to Jerusalem," – this course alone could leave him not only with head unbowed but with the sublime sense of having conquered in himself all the forces the world could bring against him. This alone could lift his life to a level higher than any it had reached before and make its meaning for mankind at once wonderful, and terrible, and unescapable. And so he chose it. And if this be "selfishness," then I declare it a holy selfishness, and I call for more of it. And I promise that every man who yields himself to its self-consuming passion shall in his measure exalt the life of the race.

But you would misunderstand me if you thought for a moment that I am preaching indifference to others and disregard of their need in the interest of the individual's fulfilling himself. I admit that what I am saying could be expressed in these terms, and he who had ears for it would understand it aright. But for most people it would be completely misleading. I tell you that when I hear most people talk about self-realization, something in me winces. For the self-realization I care about is suggested better by some other word altogether, and can never be reached by any man with his eye constantly on his own development. No, never! The man I am talking about now is one whose whole life is lived for the human race, who knows himself one with his kind, and for its sake consumes himself. In the last analysis, their life is his life, and his life their life – so much so that it is when he is truest to himself that he most completely denies himself and makes his richest gift to society; and it is when he is most entirely lost in the highest farthest love that he himself is most completely satisfied. And it is just as unescapable now as it was the day it was said first: he who would find his life, must lose it. Paradoxes? Yes! Without them no one can get far in the whole realm of life about which I am talking. Here the truest selfishness is the highest altruism, and the most far-reaching altruism requires the sternest trueness to oneself.

Probably more people would hold out against pity if Christian teaching had not so long exalted it as an ideal, and if this idealization of it as something admirable and Christ-like had not blinded people to what it actually is.

Pity is stooping to weakness. Pity is letting the plane and the pitch of one's life be determined by reference to another's fears, or dependence, or blindness, or smallness, or to the suffering of the diseased and the degenerate. He who takes pity on the weak accepts into himself the weakness of the man whom he pities, and lets himself down to that man's level. He who allows himself to be torn too much over the suffering of the weak, the beaten and the broken, only thereby swells the sea of suffering already flooding the world, and without any compensatory gain. Pity means the infection of the well with the weakness of the sick.

It means more than that. It means that the weakness of the weak is preserved. Pity prevents the elimination of human waste. To be sure, we need those who will be like a master gardener, who will choose our goals and decide which kinds of life would mark an advance and should be striven toward, and which kinds should be got rid of, but nothing should be allowed to interfere with the free play of forces by which those unable to step forward with the rest are exposed and brought down. Pity as we have it interferes with the process of natural selection by which life has ever weeded out those for whom the pace is too stiff. It puts security above significance, and the mere continuation of the species above the advance, at least on the part of its most favored members, into ever higher realms of experience. It has brought it about that today, as Nietzsche pointed out, our society is like an organism that has lost the strength to excrete its own waste. So long have we heard that the strong should bear the burdens of the weak, that almost everyone is either sick or some sick person's nurse. Our life centers around disease. Many of our most capable people are spending their powers on trying to salvage human wreckage, on all sorts of life that can never come to anything, and not even on salvaging it, but only on preserving it, on merely keeping alive by artificial means that which ought to die, and which, if left to nature, would die. Witness our imbeciles, our incurables and defectives of all kinds. We are become like a cow stabled in its own dung, and these doers of good are piling the dung higher and higher about the animal's head till it is almost asphyxiated in its own filth. We are nurturing the weeds in our garden till the vegetables and flowers threaten to be smothered out of existence.

I say: he who acts out of pity for another's weakness puts that weakness in himself. I say: he who acts out of pity for another's weakness helps to keep that weakness on the earth. Pity means – the retention of weakness, and the spread of it. But over against this I declare that out of weakness can come no good whatever. To be sure, weakness on one side may to some extent be offset by strength on another. A great mind or soul may reside in a frail body, and call forth our admiration the more because it has triumphed over physical handicap. Also a body or mind that has been shattered under the relentless drive of a dedicated and dauntless will, like a spear from the thrust of a mighty arm, is different from a body which is defective congenitally, which is fed on bad blood. But in weakness itself there is no good whatever.

The due fate of weakness in human life is to be recognized for what it is, and to be accepted as the mark of inferiority. It is the evidence of some deficiency of vitality, of lack of power to see, to do, to bear, to invent, to coordinate, to synthesize – lack of power of some sort. If the human race is to advance toward ever higher ends, its weakness must ever be in the process of being sloughed off. In every age the weakest part should be eliminated. Therefore, I do *not* say, Let a man set his pace to the pace of the weak. I say rather, Let him run that grandest race that is in him. Let him be a challenge to the very strongest, if he can, that they fly yet farther and higher. And so far as the weak are concerned, let him not accept their weakness, or if it be forced upon him, then let him under no circumstances stoop to it. Rather let his deed and his word be a challenge to them to measure up to his strength, to match his deed of strength with a deed of strength of their own. If they rise to the challenge and do match strength with strength, the gain for life is obvious. And if, on the other hand, they cannot, if they try, and fail, and in the failure fall and are broken and as wreckage are eliminated – well, here also, to the eye capable of rising above softness and falseness, above pity and sentiment, the gain for life is obvious again. Whatever the response of the weak, whether they are made stronger or succumb, the result for life is gain. But he who acts out of pity betrays his own highest possibilities, and commits a crime against the highest life of mankind. Nietzsche was right. He who succors human weakness, commits against the highest life of mankind what is no less than a crime.

We know this. Every thinking man knows this. If the human race is to achieve the high ends we would set before it, the weakness in it must go – our weakest members, and the weaknesses in our strongest members. We know this, but we have refused to face it. We have refused to face it because our religion has made us weak. I am not blind to the cruelty of our age, but in the very realm of our aspirations, in the very realm where we reach what we believe our highest, we are emasculated. We have emasculated our conception of Jesus who has figured for our world as its ideal. For me there are things about him which can only be described as terrible. But we have made him into a womanish man. We have exalted greatness till it has left us soft, and love till it has made us sentimental, and practical help to the weak and in the alleviation of all pain till it has become the distinctive Christian virtue. We regard suffering with a veritable horror. We have made an ideal of harmlessness, of hurting no one, and our utopia and our heaven are places where there is to be no pain.

But it shall not be so – for life is not so. The truly wise in every age have known that the thing to fear is not suffering – not even causing it, but only that untrueness to one's own highest vision in which life is betrayed and lost. They have known that pain is an element inherent in all life on this earth, that our sublimest men have been they who have suffered most, and that probably it shall continue to be so so long as life on this earth shall go on.

We need to summon ourselves, therefore, to a new hardiness. Ye have heard that it hath been said, Let the strong bear the burdens of the weak. But I say to you, Let the strong set a pace which the weak *cannot* follow. Ye have heard that it hath been said, Have pity on the weaker brothers. But I say to you, Let your love be rather to the heroes and the titans of the race, to the sublimest and most godlike ones, where your love cannot be pity but instead is fellow-suffering, which you can share because you also have known profound suffering, which you bore willingly, and for long, for love's sake, for the sake of love and mankind, and which you would bear again, and forever, for mankind's sake.

We have seen many start to follow their stars. And we have seen most of those who started gradually succumb to one or another of the obstacles and seductions of which I have written. But to the one of which I wish to write now succumb nearly all of the few who have got safely thus far. It is the concern for effectiveness. It is the psychology of "success." It is the desire to bring about some tangible and immediate change in the environment under which one's fellow men are suffocated and crushed; the desire to gain recognition, to have influence or to hold a following. This is a seduction which takes him whose intelligence is keen, whose love is deep, and whose dedication is unto death.

He is the kind of man who says, "For me it is not enough to put salve on the sores. It is not enough to support bread lines and settlements in slums and to resist war. I want to root out the system which produces this slavery and which makes war inevitable. I must be a reformer." He may even say, "I must become a communist." And such a man I respect, as I never can respect those who make out of helping others a profession, and a good name, and a comfortable living. And I recognize also and full well that our economic system, and the political situation which grows out of it, continually have to be changed, that all the external structures of human society have to be modified, that they were all made for man and not man for them, and that whenever men have outgrown their institutions, their institutions must be changed to meet the new human need, even as the shell which long supported the life of the chick must give way when the life of the chick has become too large any longer to be contained in the old shell. And I know this means that there must be those who will work out what changes are required and who will provide humanity with leadership in that direction. And so long as a man can devote himself to reform (or revolution) in the social set-up without compromise with his highest vision, it seems to me that this is where he belongs and that his work is very necessary and valuable. And what I am saying now against being concerned for effectiveness is really not addressed to this sort of man at all. He has found his niche and is filling it.

But there is another kind of man – the man of artist-temperament, the man who is ahead of his time, whose vision is beyond the reach of the masses, the man who in all his highest holiest hours feels that there has been laid upon him a word of his own to utter, a deed of his own to do, and that in the sheer living of his own honest life lies the greatest gift to his fellow men of which his particular life is capable. But the first few steps toward making that gift reveal to him that his generation has no ears for his truth and no eyes for his beauty. He sees that its god is neither truth, nor beauty, nor love. Long ago hath it succumbed to the spirit of the Ford factory. It worships the machine. Its god is effectiveness, the visibly, tangibly, immediately effective. And he too *wants* to have an effect. Out of his very love for his fellow men he cares that so many of them should plow and plant and another reap, that so many of them should build houses and another live in them. He longs for a world in which they shall all be born with an access to opportunity proportionate to their capacities to use it. He cares. And because he cares so deeply, he wants to see things changed. But he soon discovers that effectiveness in bringing about external social change — the primary objective of all the "social gospelites" — requires a meshing of one's life into the very ordinary life of men about him which it is impossible to square with his ideals. He must decide whether he is going to live his life for the sake of the effect of it, or whether he is child enough and fool enough to be content with sheer honesty, with simply living the life that belongs to him *regardless* of its effect — or, its *lack* of effect. He must choose between effectiveness and — trueness. He must. It cannot be both. And the tragedy is that so many of those who have got thus far, who have been faithful to their One Beloved until now, finally succumb to the spiritual uncleanness of the crowd and go a-whoring after Results.

But this kind of man, because he has struggled through faithfully thus far, *so* far, and because he draws my love to him, I would urge to be of strong courage, to keep faith in himself. He must not let the blindness of the world to the truth and the beauty and the significance of what are within him blind him to it also. How often hath beauty had to wait for the birth of lovers that would be worthy of her. Let him keep faith with his vision.

And let him not be deceived. No man can keep his eye quite single so long as he is constantly thinking of his life in terms of its effect on other people or institutions, and always steering and calculating for such. For, while he may have one eye which is ever sensitive for truth, he has to have another eye with which he is constantly looking for what will be effective. He cannot think singly of what is true, he must always be asking himself how much of what he now sees to be true it is expedient to say, how much of what he really believes, it is possible to do without so alienating people that they will not follow him. But these two eyes look in different directions, and so long as a man is concerned about the effects of his life he cannot escape becoming at last spiritually cross-eyed!

And worse than that – whenever a man gets into the fatal habit of playing fast and loose with his light, following it or not following it according as it may promise to produce some result which he desires, he necessarily begins to go blind. For, as I have already said, the inexorable law is, Use your eyes or lose them. He becomes what practically all those become whose purpose is not first of all to live themselves, but to promote life in others, to help them, to serve them, to do them good, to "save" them, all those would-be shepherds who are always ready to sacrifice their integrity in order to keep the sheep at their heels. They become blind leaders of the blind, and in the end the influence they did so much to keep proves to be worthless. They keep their following, but they lead – nowhere!

After all, who *is* the most effective man? Perhaps it just is not he who is most concerned about it, who strains for it most. Seventy-five years ago Henry Ward Beecher, Phillips Brooks, and Colonel Ingersol – great talkers all of them – were drawing enormous crowds to hear them speak. At the same time there was Henry David Thoreau, who for about two years lived alone at Walden Pond, and here learned to gaze so deeply into the inner meaning and reality of life that thereafter he could write down in his journal great thoughts that lie across the pathway of mankind like boulders. To be sure, at one time, believing that slavery was a thing of moral enormity, he refused to pay taxes to the state of Massachusetts that supported it, and in consequence went to jail. Yet, for the most part, Thoreau lived a very quiet life, and if people in those days had been asked who was going to have the most far-reaching influence, the men whose names I mentioned first or Thoreau, I doubt if many could have been found who would have cast their vote for Thoreau. And yet, years later, when Gandhi is searching for the idea and the practice by which to break the power of British imperialism in India, he goes to Henry David Thoreau's idea of civil disobedience. And evidence still comes in that Thoreau's influence is ever widening and deepening, and that he who is already accounted America's greatest maker of epigrams will yet be recognized, ahead even of Emerson, as the foremost seer and prophet that has come out of New England. For while possibly Emerson wrote better, Thoreau did better. He did not compromise. He put trueness above goodness. It meant more to him to live sincerely than to gain a hearing or to be received in society. All that he wrote came out of what he already had done. Therefore nothing he wrote has to be discounted in the light of his life. Rather his life confirms and seals all that he so pungently, pointedly said. Innermost vision, life, and word, all fit together. He was an undivided whole. And this it is – wholeness – all parts pulling together to the nod of one inner coxswain at the helm – this it is that gives a man the greatest influence of which his life is capable.

In the long run must it not ever be so? How *can* a man have his greatest effect when (as it were) he is constantly cramping his natural expression? How can he stand off and hit the world with his whole force so long as he keeps one arm tied to his side? How can he have room in which to swing on it when he is squeezing himself into some tight cubby-hole of a position which presses in upon him as closely as the walls of a coffin? Perhaps, by his compromise with his vision, he may make more of an immediate impression than another man who simply keeps faith with himself. But does it last? That is the question. Does it last? Does it go deep? I believe that no man shall ever come to the place where he can leave his most lasting mark upon the unfolding life of the race until he has achieved a supreme indifference to what men think of him. He will have the lofty indifference of a mountain. The mountain does not ask to be recognized as a mountain. It is one, and men cannot escape it. They may climb over it or tunnel under it, but they cannot ignore it. Their whole life is altered because it is there.

I have said already – but lest you forget it I say again – I know that there must be those who are like channel-buoys by which canal-boats and tug-boats find their way in and out of a harbor – that is, those by whom society can find its way through a particular tangled situation in a given age. These men are the statesmen and reformers. But I say we need also, and more desperately than anything else, those men who will not reform anything, who will be simply light, through whose lives the reformers will see that changes are needed, and what changes, and be fired to try to bring those changes to pass. Those men are like stars hung in the sky from which men never can escape. They are ever luring the hardiest souls, the most dauntless mariners, farther and farther out from shore, to venture at last "where man has never yet dared to go" and there to "risk the ship, themselves, and all." Not that any man by trying can ever become a star. More than anything else, such an aspiration is likely to put out whatever light there was in him. And yet no one ever knows how far one's faithfulness to one's highest vision in one's own corner is going to have influence. Before ever there was a Jesus there was a John the Baptist, and before there was a John the Baptist there must have been many young people around Palestine whose spirits were on fire. At their flame John the Baptist lit the light which in his hands became a torch, and which, passed on, in Jesus' hands became a star, and passed still further on, may in time become a sun. The very names of these young people were long ago forgotten, but except for their faithfulness there would have been no Jesus.

Perhaps the truth of the matter is that I, who have so much to say about the poisonous and seductive concern for effects, am really the one who cares about effects most. Perhaps I have spoken as I have because I care so much that men should not fail of their greatest effect. I see how through the centuries men have been deceived by their near-sightedness. Misled by their impatience, by their obsession with the immediate and the external, by their blindness as to what is real and enduring, they have spent themselves in vain, over and over again. To measure results truly one must have an eye that can pierce through the deceptive sheen and glamour of appearances to the quiet core of enduring fact and force within. One must have an eagle-eye of long range, and perch on a high mountain with the centuries stretched out far below. Then one sees how the noisy and the spectacular in the past has quickly subsided until in the present there is hardly so much as a ripple of it left. And, on the other hand, certain words and deeds in the present, that seem almost as intangible as light and song, almost as defenseless as a new-born babe, slowly come to be spiritual earth and sun for a whole race of men far into the future. Long and long have I believed — at last it is getting into my very blood — that the really significant changes in human society are not the changes that strike the eye and the ear of man. You put a nation through the throes of a revolution and at last dress it up in a new social order according to your idea of what is good, but how often only to realize in the end that underneath the apparent change the men and women in your new social order remained pretty much what they were. Somewhat as the monkey, even after you have pulled a fulldress suit on him, and stuck a cane in his hand, and a high hat on his head, still remains – a monkey. The evils bear new names and take new forms but remain the same evils. The really profound and far-reaching changes, out of which in time the need and the demand for the external changes come, are the slow, invisible and intangible changes in men's ideas and ideals. "The movements that guide the world," said Nietzsche, "come on doves' feet." "Around the devisers of new values revolveth the world: - invisibly it revolveth. But around the actors revolve the people and the glory; such is the course of things." We continually say, but how very rarely really believe, what is surely the great fact, that "the Kingdom of God cometh not with observation." It does not come in the things that we can see. It *stealeth* over the world.

To him, therefore, who has the soul of the artist, whose chief gift to his fellow men is simply himself, is simply in being out and out what he really is deep down inside – to him I would draw near that I may whisper to him my very soul in this matter. I would say to him, "be like the dancer. The dancer can bring his dance to the last turn of perfection and have his greatest effect on his spectators precisely when he has completely forgotten not only himself but even those who watch him. He is utterly lost in his dance. He *is* the dance. And do you likewise forget all else but your vision. Let is possess you – utterly. Clothe it in your own flesh and blood. Let it walk the earth in you. And the effect of it – what men make of it – forget it! Only then will it have its greatest effect. Not they do most for the Kingdom of God who talk about 'advancing it'. They do most for the Kingdom of God who see that it *is*, and *live* in it."

IV. *A Regimen for Spiritual Pregnancy*

Thus far we have been concerned with some of the obstacles and seductions which, negatively, we must avoid lest we be lured from our path or brought to our knees. I wish now to speak along a more positive line. Both women and men must know what it is to be spiritually pregnant, to be swollen with a life within them which they cannot contain, and to which they must give birth though they die for it. I want to bring to your attention some of the things which I think very important if this life within us is to be brought to birth and not to a miscarriage. Let me lay before you a hygiene for spiritual pregnancy.

First of all, though it is a thing which has been implicit in all I have said, *Be true*. I do not talk about truth. After all I believe there is no such thing. Or if there be, no one has ever known what it is, nor, I venture to say, ever will. Truth! What *is* truth? Truth is the cloud-veiled summit of earth's highest mountain which men approach from every side, yet never see. Nor indeed is it necessary, for within every one of us is that sense of where our highest life lies, to which we need only to be undeviatingly faithful In order to come out perhaps slowly yet surely upon solid ground.

With this relativistic attitude toward truth, men are very apt to yield to the temptation to trifle with their light. They say, "There is no truth. It is only a matter of your conception of it, and my conception of it. I cannot be sure that mine is absolutely sound. Why should I take it too seriously?" But such an attitude is proving spiritually devastating. Just because we know no *absolute* truth, just because there *is* no external authority upon which we may rely, all the more is it necessary that a man should be terribly obedient to that highest vision of truth which he has within himself. Only he who does that, will know what it is to get out of the fog through which most men today grope and out of the swamp in which they flounder. Only he will get his feet on solid ground, and see surely the way he must go.

As aids to keeping on one's own path, I wish to say three things. The first one is, Do not resist evil. Now this is an instance of what I would not say to everyone. By most men evil had better be resisted with all the strength they have in them. But to him who knows what it is to have a life of his own, a word of his own to utter and a deed of his own to do, who has it in him to create, to him I do say and can hardly say too often, Do not resist evil. I say that Tolstoy and Gandhi do not go far enough. It is not merely a matter of not resisting evil with evil, and violence with violence. For this man it is necessary to avoid resisting it at all. Better that he stop up his ears against it and close his eyes to it than that he should allow his life to be turned into a mere resistance to it. I say to him, Do not let that holy thing which is your life be drawn down and degraded into mere negative opposition. Do not let your activity in the world take its departure from what men call its evil, lest your life become but a reflex thing, a mere matter of a reaction to something outside yourself, a reply, a come-back, an attempt at a solution or reform – a mere thing of tinkering, patching, doctoring. It may often be good to *re-form* some old thing which has gone to pieces, but it can never compare with the new and living and inwardly self-directing form to which he who has long been pregnant can give birth as a mother gives to the earth new life in the form of her child. I say, Beware lest your best energy be drawn off and wasted in all that is negative – in resentment, rebellion, criticism, and bitterness. I say, As you value your life, as you revere that within you which can create, hold yourself to the positive. Be like the spring which forever bubbles forth from within. Be like the sun which does not bemoan the clouds but ever from within pours forth light and warmth. Do not try to reform but dare to walk the earth in your own simple manhood, in the faith that wherever a *man* goes the latent manhood of those around him rises up in response.

I say next, Let us have it clearly understood with ourselves from the outset that we are going to put our life ahead of our living. First we are going to say out the thing we believe most true. We are going to do the thing which to the bottom of us we believe most worth doing. And for our bread and butter we will get along – somehow! And likewise with our courses in college, with our aspirations for degrees or advancements in the career on which we are started. We will make room for our life. If this comes to mean that we must neglect a course till we "flunk" it, or lighten our academic load, or leave college altogether, we will do it. No matter where or how we are situated, we will undertake so to arrange our life that we shall have time and energy for those things which will bring us closer and closer to a true knowledge of ourselves and get us started on the kind of life which flows from the very center of our being. Whatever interferes with that will have to go. We will make room for our life.

And then, as the third aid to keeping on one's own true path, I have to say, Learn what it is to be hard. I would remind you that another man once said, "Except ye hate – father, mother, wife and child, brother and sister, and your own life also," Not that either man meant so much either to hate or be hard (for they were both men of tender heart) as they mean to whet the edge of "No man can serve two masters," and "If thine eye be single, thy whole body shall be full of light." And they found it necessary to press right into the viscera of shrinking human flesh the point of the necessity to put first things first. They knew that no seer had ever been fool enough to turn men loose with the mere injunction to love. They knew that love was not love at all, that it became but a betrayal of love at its highest, but a matter of softness and sentiment, unless it had direction and kept on edge. They were insisting with one voice, "Thou shalt love the Lord thy God with all thy heart, and with all thy soul, and with all thy strength and with all thy mind – with all the passion of thy being." But – thy God is not my God, and my God is not thy God, nor the God of any one of us the God of any other of us. For each and all of us, his God is that highest, holiest thing he knows. To that, let him be true – even though he die for it. And everything else will take care of itself.

One of the most important matters for the full growth of the deepest life within us is what I might call our spiritual diet. Much depends on what we feed this life. And here my word is: let a man find for himself kingly fare. Let him turn to the great seers of the race and sit at their feet long and reverently. Let him seek out those whose life and words reach the deepest understanding in him and quicken it to yet deeper understanding. Let Dionysus greet Dionysus, the god in them speaking to the god in him.

And this is no counsel to subservience. It is true indeed that none can climb for another or see for another, and that once a man accepts another man's light for his own, he becomes a satellite and forfeits the possibility of becoming a sun, of having a course of his own, and of knowing the high fellowship of fellow suns and creators. But it is true also that we are not the first ones to seek the spring that we seek, nor the first to travel the path that leads to it. The path is our own so much that even if no one had ever traveled it before us, we should have to travel it now. But it *has* been traveled before, and again and again. And those who have traveled it have gone to the pains to set up signposts by which those who come after may avoid false turns, and they have left careful records of landmarks they found along the way and of grand vistas their eyes gazed upon, by which one is assured, when one finds one's own eyes sweeping the same far horizon, that one stands where once they stood. And there is no reason why we who come after should not benefit by the experience of those who have gone before: there is every reason why we should. It was in no small part for us, and others like us, that they marked the trail so carefully, and it is simply false to pretend that life is all one vast unexplored wilderness and to hunt for our spring as though the trail to it had not already been blazed. The spring which eternally pours forth life for man, and the waters of which satisfy his deepest thirst – that spring has been found. It was found long ago, and the way to it marked. And if the thirst in us is real and desperate, if we feel that somehow we must find that water or verily we shall die, then surely from the first man we meet who has been to that spring and drunk of that water, we shall seek all the direction, counsel, and encouragement that he can give. This is what all the seers before us have done. In the years of their own seeking, they turned to those before them who had sought and found. To do otherwise would be to reveal that in our hearts we cared less about finding life than about maintaining an appearance of self-sufficiency.

For long close contact with these men, though sometimes extremely painful, will prove very salutary. Often they may be like a daily dip into acid, burning out of us all that was dross and counterfeit. All of them will hold before us a mirror in which we catch the lineaments of our own souls. They will save us from wasting years of our lives floundering in bogs and following paths that would take us nowhere. And they will become our comrades. These men, though dead, for us will live. And thereafter, though no one walks by our side, we can never be really alone.

So I have found it. For years I saturated myself in the life of one great seer after another, each in his turn almost to the temporary exclusion of all others. As it happened Jesus came first, but Buddha, Vivekananda and Gandhi soon followed, and Kabir, and then the great modern giants of the West, Thoreau and Whitman, and Blake and Nietzsche. Without failing to reserve to myself the final decision as to what was true, or in any case as to what did or did not belong to me, I simply laid myself open to these men and exposed myself to the full force of their life and thought. And what I feel I owe to them is quite beyond what I can express in words. The evidence of it must be found, if at all, in my life.

And in consequence I hold it of the utmost importance that everyone setting out to find the path to his spring, should discover those men of spiritual genius whose inspiration and direction and discipline may help him on his way. For this reason I have placed in the appendix at the end of this little work a list of those books by the great seers, or about them, which have most significantly fed my own growth. Many of them it took me years to find, and to have got some of them ten or fifteen years earlier I might well have paid with years of my life. There are a few of them which mean more to me than all the other books in existence. They are the condensed essence of the greatest souls that have walked this earth. And he may draw near to them who can.

From all I have said it must be evident that this life is not one which we can postpone until we get to some heaven or until some revolution arrives, or until some other people can go with us. It is the life which we must live here and now on this earth and in these bodies of ours and everything that vitally relates to them must be regarded with a new reverence. I like the tradition which prevailed among the old Irish that no man could be a king among them who had a physical blemish. It should be a matter of deepest shame to us that man, the crown of creation, is the sickest animal on the face of the earth. The day will come when a man who has so much as a cold will feel as ashamed as our fathers felt of sin. Just look at us, with our fallen arches, decayed teeth, bald heads, deaf ears, defective eyes – everybody sick with something. A man must set himself to find out what are the laws and the conditions by which we can cease to be the race of degenerates that we are now and become a race with bodies that are robust, clean-limbed, and beautiful.

For one thing we need to learn to put at least as much intelligence into the feeding of our own bodies and the bodies of our children as we do into the feeding of our cows. Every one knows that you can not get the most milk from a cow if you disregard the laws of its feeding. And man shall never reach his highest possibilities spiritually until he learns to put into his body food of such kind and in such quantities as have been established by science to make for health.

And likewise with light and air. We forget that our whole period of civilization is only as it were a few hours after a period in which for thousands of years the bodies of our ancestors were exposed to air and sunshine. And there is no sensible reason in the world why at least in the summer time we should not feel free to wear as few clothes as the people wear in India.

Each man's intelligence can complete the case I am making here for a new regard and reverence for the body. It is necessary now only for me to add that of course, with the position I am taking, I believe in the holiness of sex. To be sure, it can be no more beautiful than the people who enter it. But whenever a man and woman are brought together in a deep unity of soul and mind; whenever each looking deep into the eyes of the other, sees mirrored there his One Beloved, before the beauty of whom he is utterly lost, in speechless adoration, and wonder, and love; whenever they come together in spirit, before ever they come together in body, then everything that they can do the one with the other, is holy. I say that any man who says a word against the sanctity of sex lays filth at the very door of life. And I say that no man shall ever make his life holy who does not know that sex is holy.

It is necessary, next, to make it very clear that the kind of life about which I am talking is one which cannot be reached by the rational faculty – by ideas, by the power in us which reasons. To be sure there is a place for reason, a very important place, and the life I am talking about is not one in which reason will be violated, but only one by which reason can be transcended, which is quicker and surer-footed than reason, one in which all a man's perspective faculties are brought to a focus and his whole life shaped into an organic whole. Most of these rationalists – what do they remind me of? They make me think of an earthworm blindly chewing its way through the dark. They make me think of a blind man tapping his way along a sidewalk with a cane. They make me think of a man who, in order to know that ten and ten are twenty, still has to count on his fingers and toes. But in the Kingdom of God everybody dances – dances as no one can dance who has to tap his way with a cane – dances as only he can dance who is sure of the ground under his feet and sees clearly the way before him. In the life I am talking about a man has some mental arithmetic by which he knows in a flash that ten and ten are twenty, without stopping to count, without having to pass everything through the mill of his mind. He has something which in the more subtle and complex realms of human experience is like the instinct of an animal by which he knows immediately his food from his poison, his friend from his foe, and his way out of every woods. In him instinct and intuition have been marvelously married. In him instinct has been refined, and sensitized, and focused, and extended in its range. Through its voice all his highest perceptive faculties speak one integral word.

Indeed, it is necessary not only to get beyond dependence upon reason, beyond being sure by proving rather by simply seeing. It is necessary, also, to leave behind even this much-lauded thing of living by ideals, which, after all, is very closely related to that whole domination of life by the rational process against which I have been speaking. For he who lives by ideals usually works out with his head a set of abstract conceptions of what he considers morally most desirable and then takes himself by the back of the neck and tries to make himself act even as he thinks. He constructs a set of fixed rigid molds into which he tries to force his living impulses to flow. Only to discover at last that the whole experience has been worse than a failure, it has actually left his impulses deadened. He may have succeeded in putting himself through the *motions* of acting according to his ideals, and his life may be impressive for its excellence and for its consistency, but there will be in it no leap or song or radiance or power. It will be stiff and stilted, artificial, thin and strained, without any elemental force in it and behind it. For it all springs not from what he deeply feels but from what he merely thinks. He lives only from his head up. He is a plant without roots, a plant cut off from its roots, which are in his depths.

Oh, we are deeper than we know. Oh, so little do most of us so much as guess what we are, that we spend all our strength and all our days in skating aimlessly hither and thither on the veriest surface of life. But all the while every one of us is an ocean. All that we think we want is only the waves that vex this ocean's surface, where all is fret, and froth, and fickleness. But what I am talking about is like what a man would reach if he plumbed deep-deep-deep down, until he came to a great current which, with steadiness, and vastness, and in silence, moves across the ocean-floor of his life. When first we begin to think, all of us are like a glass of muddy water, and most of us, in our efforts to find out what is within us, resemble a man who would try to get the water to clear up by feverishly poking in it! and stirring it! But we all know that if we will but let the water stand perfectly still, it will become clear by itself. And so with us: if we will at last but be inwardly very still, absolutely unafraid, utterly willing to go anyway, then, marvelously, the way we should go will become clear. Every one of us, to change the figure, has in him that which is like an underground stream, which the eye never sees. But if a man goes out into the woods where it is very still and under which it flows, and lies down with his ear close to the earth, and just listens, and listens, he shall hear this river of his deepest life as it sings its way toward the sea.

Nothing I have to say is more important than this. For me it is fundamental, and central, and cardinal. In that which speaks and moves within me in the deepest stillness of my being, I have my compass for every sea, my unfailing monitor at every parting of the way. Here is my Beloved in whose embrace I can find rest and refreshment whenever loneliness, and weariness, and darkness press upon me too heavily. This is that which "sufficeth" me. With it, I can go anywhere. Without it, I would long ago have had to confess myself beaten... I say, Let men learn to be still. Let men learn to listen. You know not the day nor the hour when the Son of Man cometh. Be ready to catch the first sound of your Beloved's step on your walk. Learn to know Him no matter what the disguise under which He may present Himself at your door. With Him keep a life-long tryst, and be ever ready to steal away, no matter who the person before you or what the business at hand... into the deep silence of your mind.

Again I must caution anyone who sets out to follow his deepest life against being too sure that it can be kept within the limits of conventional morality. Let him not take it for granted that men will think him a saint or even consider him respectable. For life itself is un-moral. It has no interest in our moral codes. Our "good" and our "evil" are merely labels which a given society has placed upon certain *kinds* of life. Each society's Ten Commandments (or the equivalent thereof) is a merely human evaluation in which it holds up before its members certain ways of feeling and thinking and doing which, no matter how much contradicted by the codes of its neighbors, it believes with passionate earnestness to be essential to the advancement of its life. All those who conform to this moral code (they are the great commonplace average) are considered good and virtuous – in this society. Whereas, everyone who falls below this average is pronounced evil, as a criminal is considered evil. But, and no less certainly, will every man who rises above this average be pronounced evil, even as Socrates was condemned as a corrupter of the youth, and as Jesus was cast out because he stirred up the people. In every generation life comes onto the stage like a herd of young mustangs. But they no more than arrive than society's cowboys jump on their backs to try to break them in, and force them to take the bit. And those who do take the bit are the "good" people! But the man who is true to his own good and evil, which belong to him as do his own blood and bone, and which fit him as he is fitted by his own skin.

Indeed, he may not only have to be called evil, he may have to do evil. I mean, do injury. In the wake of every great creative soul there are those who have been more or less broken by the way he went. Look at the sun. Now it is good that we have the sun. Without it there could be no life upon this earth. And yet for the plant that has short roots the sun is the worst thing in the world; and for a man caught in the desert without water, the sun is his most deadly enemy. And I do not doubt at all that while Jesus' setting out on eagle-wing to soar high over the deepest abysses must have started many other men at trying to fly in the same grand way, there must yet have been lots of other people, having mere stubs of wings, whose ventures to fly only resulted in fatal crashes. And yet, it is good that we have the sun, and it is good that men like Jesus should continue coming along to maintain holy among men the tradition that man is an animal that was meant to fly, an animal that can fly, and who keep men, no matter how many times they crash, forever and ever trying to fly.

So, finally, I come to that which I would say first, and in the middle, and the last, for all the way through it is of fundamental importance. No man shall know this life except as he feeds into the flame of his highest vision everything that he has. We are like a candle which can have light and give light only as it feeds into the flame its very self. The light burns on but the candle gets smaller and smaller. By the light within us we see something to do which we know will cost us our job, and upon that job wife and child are dependent. And we are afraid, and we refused to do it; only to discover that every day we delay, the flame in us burns lower. At last, afraid that if we are not obedient the flame will go out, we take this deed from which we shrink and, as it were, lay it in the flame. Then the flame burns a bit more brightly, and by its rays we see something further to do, and this time it will cost us not only our job but the friendship of the person whom we love more than anyone else on this earth. And before the prospect of it our whole being seems to shrivel up, in fear and anguish. We say we can not, we will not, do it. We absolutely refuse. And like Jonah we flee to the very ends of the earth, in a hope to escape... only to realize at last that, go where we may, we but carry with us every minute the secret sense that our light is burning lower, and lower, and lower. Until, at last, desperate, lest our light go out altogether, and in an utter agony of dedication, we gather this thing also in our hands and lay it in the flame. And so it goes on, year after year. In the end, if our flame is to be kept burning, we shall have had to feed into it everything that we have. And it often seems that it cannot reach its most ineffable beauty or attain to its most strangely piercing power until it has fed on our very blood. But let us not profane the thing with any whining about "sacrifice." No one ever yet gave up anything for the sake of the highest truth and beauty that were in him without getting far more than he gave. He is like a man seeking goodly pearls who, having found one, in his joy went and sold all that he had that he might possess himself of that pearl. And I believe that deep deep down everyone of us is secretly hoping and seeking for that which is great enough, true enough, beautiful enough, to give to it everything that he has. Deep down it is not suffering we fear. We do not fear even death. What we really fear most is that we may go through life and never find that to which we may give our all. Really everyone of us longs to erect an altar in his heart, and on it to lay down his very own self. Except we die we shall not live. And ah, how we want to live! how we want really to live!

V. *Where Is the Handful of Sticks?*

Why have I talked like this, in this extreme sort of way? Well, perhaps in part because of some secret certainty that after all it is not so extreme as it is merely unusual to the ordinary ear – or because I no longer know how to speak from my heart in any other way. But really, at bottom, it is because wherever I go I am looking for those who have ears for this kind of music. For I want to see a fire kindled on this earth, and I must try to find the dry hard fuel which the flame ever loveth. I am looking for him who has grown into a new roughness, and untamedness, and wickedness. I am looking for him who at heart is a warrior, who never knows when he has had enough, who never knows when he is beaten and who therefore never is beaten. I love him whom a dream hath possessed, and who thereafter knoweth not how to live on this earth at all, except to be hand and feet to it, and eyes and tongue to it! I love him who is filled with a divine impatience, who cannot wait to go to some heaven or for some revolution to come around the corner, but must take the whole living glory of life as he sees it and struggle to incarnate it here and now, even though it be in the face of a society set dead against him! I love him who knows what it is to be drunken, but drunk with a drunkenness that leaves no bad taste in the morning! I love him who at heart is a gambler, but for whom it is not enough to stake nickels, or dollars, even though it be dollars by the thousand or million, but who has found that which for him is so real that he stands ready not only to stake but even to lose everything that he has, and in the very losing to laugh! I love him who is a child, him who is a fool, him who is reckless and spendthrift of himself! I love those who ever come like Pied Pipers, ever luring men, bewitching men, enchanting men, by the music of their song, and by the irresistibleness of their dance, away from the walled village where life is so safe and stuffy and shut-in, to strip themselves, to set before themselves the highest heights, knowing no height high enough to pitch their tents; knowing the highest height only as a point from which to take off on outspread wings, to soar in the golden rays of the sun!

I want to see a fire kindled on this earth, and this is the kind of fuel it will take. It may have to be a very small fire but it matters not so long as its flame be one of unspeakable beauty and great steadiness. But it is difficult to keep one stick burning alone, on the snow, in the face of an icy wind. Yet with just a handful of sticks one can sometimes start quite a fire. It has already so happened on this earth more than once. But where is the handful of sticks? Where are those few who are willing to burn, and to be burnt up, in order that there may be light in this night, and warmth in this coldness? Where is the fuel which the flame ever loveth, ever longeth to lick with its love, and to make one with itself? Where is the handful of sticks?

For Further Reading †

I. TOWARD AN UNDERSTANDING OF SOME OF THE GREAT SEERS.

1. Ancient

Jesus, Man of Genius – J. Middleton Murry. (Harpers, N.Y.)
The Creed of Christ – Edmond Holmes. (Dodd, Mead, N.Y.)
Buddhism – Rhys Davids. (Macmillan, N.Y.)
Buddha and the Gospel of Buddhism – Ananda Coomaraswamy. (Putnam, N.Y.)
The Creed of Buddha – Edmond Holmes. (Dodd, Mead, N.Y.)
Aspects of the Vedanta – a series of essays, mostly by Hindus. (G.A. Natesan, Madras, India.)
Muhammad the Prophet – Maulava Muhammad Ali. (Ahmadiyya Anjuman-I-Isha'at-I-Islam, Lahore, India.)
Religions and Philosophies of the East – John M. Kennedy. (T. Werner Laurie, London.)

† Those books which the author thinks most significant for the kind of life presented in this book he has marked with an asterisk (*). A longer and more fully classified list can be obtained for fifteen cents by addressing him at Prattsville, New York.

Cosmic Consciousness – Richard Maurice Bucke. (Dutton, N.Y.)

2. *Modern*

WILLIAM BLAKE:
** *Poetry and Prose of William Blake*. Ed. By Geoffrey Keynes, 1 vol. and 3 vols. 1927. (Nonesuch Press, London.) The only reliable text. The three-volume edition has excellent reproductions of Blake's pictures
Engraved Designs of William Blake – Laurence Binyon. (Scribers, N.Y.) About one hundred reproductions of Blake's engravings. This, and Figgis' book, to be found in large libraries.
Paintings of William Blake – Darrel Figgis. (Scribners, N.Y.)
The Life of William Blake – Alexander Gilchrist. 2 vols. (John Lane, London.)
William Blake – Arthur Symons. (Constable, London, 1907.)
William Blake, A Critical Essay – Algernon Charles Swinburne. (Scribners, N.Y.)
William Blake, Poet and Mystic – Pierre Berger. (Dutton, N.Y.)
An Introduction to the Study of Blake – Max Plowman. (Dutton, N.Y.)
The Divine Vision: Blake's Vision of the Book of Job (21 illustrations) – Joseph Wicksteed. (Dutton, N.Y.)
William Blake: His Philosophy and Symbols – S. Foster Damon. (Houghton Mifflin, Boston.)
On the Minor Prophecies of William Blake – Emily S. Hamblen. (Dutton, N.Y.) 1930.

HENRY DAVID THOREAU:
All his works are worth study, but especially:
**Walden* – (Houghton Mifflin, Boston.)
Excursions – (Houghton Mifflin, Boston.)
Miscellanies – (Houghton Mifflin, Boston.)
The Heart of Thoreau's Journal – ed. by Odell Shapard. (Houghton Mifflin, Boston.)
Familiar Letters of Thoreau – F.B. Sanborn. (Houghton Mifflin, Boston.)
The Life of Henry David Thoreau – H.S. Salt. (Walter Scott, London.)
Henry Thoreau, as Remembered by A Young Friend – Edward Waldo Emerson. (Houghton Mifflin, Boston.)
Henry David Thoreau: The Man Who Escaped from the Herd – Charles Finger. (Little Blue Book, Girard, Kansas.)

WALT WHITMAN:
***Leaves of Grass.* Best edition by Emory Holloway. (Doubleday, N.Y.)
Prose Works. (David McKay, Philadelphia, Pa.)
***A Life of Walt Whitman* – Harold B. Binns. (Methuen, London.)
Days with Walt Whitman – Edward Carpenter. (Allen & Unwin, London.)
With Walt Whitman in Camden – Horace Troubel. 3 vols. (Mitchell Kennerley, N.Y.)
Whitman – Emory Holloway. (Knopf, N.Y.) Based on completest sources.
Whitman, A Study – John Burroughs. (Houghton Mifflin, Boston.)
Abraham Lincoln and Walt Whitman – Wm. E. Barton. Bobbs Merrill.) For an unfavorable impression.

Whitman and Burroughs, Comrades – Clara Barton. (Houghton Mifflin, Boston.)
Walt Whitman: Bard of the West – Emily S. Hamblen. (Little Blue Book, Girard, Kansas.)

FRIEDRICH NIETZSCHE:
Nietzsche should be faced by every thinking person over twenty-five years of age. All his work deserves careful study, preferably in the order in which it was written. The most significant of his books are the following:
The Future of our Educational Institutions – (Macmillan, N.Y.)
*The Dawn of Day – (Macmillan, N.Y.)
**The Joyful Wisdom – (Macmillan, N.Y.)
**Thus Spake Zarathustra – (Macmillan, N.Y. Also Modern Library.) One of the few greatest books in the world.
*Beyond Good and Evil – (Macmillan, N.Y. Also Modern Library.)
*The Genealogy of Morals – (Macmillan, N.Y. Also Modern Library.)
**The Will to Power – (Macmillan, N.Y.) 2 vols.
**The Twilight of the Idols – (Macmillan, N.Y.)
*Ecce Homo – (Macmillan, N.Y. Also the Modern Library.) Nietzsche's autobiography.
*Selected Letters of Friedrich Nietzsche – Edited by Oscar Levy (Doubleday Doran, Garden City, N.Y.)
*Life of Friedrich Nietzsche – Frau Förster-Nietzsche. (Macmillan, N.Y.) 2 vols.
**Life of Friedrich Nietzsche – Daniel Halévy. (T. Fisher Unwin, London.)
Friedrich Nietzsche, His Life and Work – M.A. Mügge. (Brrentano, N.Y.) Contains an excellent bibliography.

Who Is to Be Master of the World – Anthony M. Ludovici. (T.N. Foulis, London). Perhaps the best introduction, though the two following also are good.
The Gospel of Superman – Henri Lichtenberger. (Macmillan, N.Y.)
Friedrich Nietzsche and His New Gospel – Emily S. Hamblen. (Richard Badger, Gorham Press, Boston.)
Friedrich Nietzsche – George Burman Foster. (Macmillan, N.Y.) Best introduction to Nietzsche for those with Christian background.
Friedrich Nietzsche, the Dionysian Spirit of the Age – A.R. Orage. (T.N. Foulis, London.)
The Dance of Siva – Ananda Coomaraswamy. (The Sunrise Turn, Inc, New York City.) The chapter entitled, "A Cosmopolitan View of Nietzsche."
Friedrich Nietzsche – George Brandes. (Heinemann, London.)
Quintessence of Nietzsche – John M. Kennedy. (T. Werner Laurie, London.)
Nietzsche the Thinker – William H. Salter. (Holt, N.Y.)
The Philosophy of Nietzsche – A. Wolf. (Constable, London.)
Friedrich Nietzsche – Emily S. Hamblen. (Little Blue Book, Girard, Kansas.)

RAMAKRISHNA and VIVEKANANDA:
The Life and Sayings of Ramakrishna – Max Miller. (Longmans, N.Y.)
The Master as I Saw Him – Sister Nivedita. Reminiscences of Vivekananda. (Longmans, London.)
Prophets of the New India – Romain Rolland. (Boni, N.Y.)

The Writings and Speeches of Vivekananda – May be obtained from The Vedanta Society, 34 West 71st Street, New York City.

II. LIVES OF OTHER SEERS AND CREATORS, ALSO OF REBELS AND REVOLUTIONISTS

Saint Joan – Bernard Shaw. (Brentano, N.Y.) Particularly the Introduction
The Journal of George Fox – Edited by Rufus Jones. (Pub. By the Friends' Book Stores, Philadelphia, Pa.)
William Lloyd Garrison – A.H. Grimke. (Funk & Wagnalls, N.Y.)
Herman Melville, Mariner and Mystic – Raymond M. Weaver. (Doran, N.Y.)
Herman Melville – Bertrand M. Wainger. (Union College Faculty Papers, Union College, Schenectady, N.Y., 1932.)
The Romance of Leonardo da Vinci – Dmitri Merejkowski. (Modern Library, N.Y.)
The Life of Olive Schreiner – S.C. Cronwright-Schreiner. (T. Fisher Unwin, London.)
Mahatma Gandhi – Romain Rolland. (Century, N.Y.)
Autobiography – M.K. Gandhi. (Navajivan Press, India.)
The books about Gandhi by C.F. Andrews are entirely reliable. They are published by Macmillan, N.Y.

III. BOOKS THAT HAVE COME OUT OF MYSTICAL EXPERIENCE, AND INSPIRATIONAL BOOKS.

The Bhagavad Gita. Translated by Edwin Arnold, entitled "The Song Celestial," is recommended by Gandhi for English readers, and it the most beautiful. (Kegan, Paul,

London.)   A more literal translation by Charles Johnson. (Quarterly Book Department, N.Y.)

**Songs of Kabir* — translated by Rabindranath Tagore. (Macmillan, N.Y.)

Gitanjali — Rabindranath Tagore. (Macmillan, N.Y.)

Wisdom of the Hindus — Edited by Brian Brown. (Brenato, N.Y.)

The Gospel of Buddha — Edited by Paul Carus.   (Open Court, Chicago.)

Tao Teh King — Lao Tzu.   Translated by Isabella Mears. (Theosophical Publishing House, London.)

The Persian Mystic — Edited by F.H. Davis.   2 small vols. (Widsom of the East series, John Murray, London.) Vol. I - Jalalu'Din Rumi. Vol. II — Jami.

The Cloud of Unknowing — Anonymous. Edited by Evelyn Underhill. (John Watkins, London.)

Theologia Germanica — Anonymous. (Macmillan, N.Y.)

The Practice of the Presence of God — Brother Lawrence. (Revell, N.Y.)

The Signature of All Things — Jacob Boehme. (Everyman Library, Dutton, N.Y.)

Centuries of Meditation — Thomas Traherne. (Ed. & pub. By Bertram Dobell. 77 Charing Cross Road, London.)

**Poetry and Prose of William Blake* — Edited by Geoffrey Keynes. (Nonesuch Press, London.)

Louis Lambert, and Seraphita — Honoré de Balzac. (Little Brown, Boston.)

A Dream of John Ball — William Morris. (Longmans, N.Y.)

**Thus Spake Zarathustra — Friedrich Nietzsche. Macmillan, N.Y.)

Essays – Ralph Waldo Emerson. (Houghton Mifflin, Boston.) Especially, perhaps, his First and Second Series, his "Self-Reliance" above all.
The Heart of Emerson's Journal – Edited by Bliss Perry. (Houghton Mifflin, Boston.)
Moby Dick – Herman Melville. (Nonesuch, N.Y.) To be read here for the profound allegory of the soul hidden in it.
Walden – Henry David Thoreau. (Houghton Mifflin, Boston.)
Leaves of Grass – Walt Whitman. (Doubleday, N.Y.)
Towards Democracy – Edward Carpenter. (Scribners, N.Y.)
Light on the Path – Mabel Collins. (Theosophical Press, Chicago.)
On Compromise – John Morley. (Macmillan, N.Y.)
Dreams – Olive Schreiner. (Little Brown, Boston.)
Stories, Dreams, and Allegories – Olive Schreiner. (Stokes, N.Y.)
The Crock of Gold – James Stephens. (Macmillan, N.Y.)
Collected Works – Padraic H. Pearse. Plays, stories, and poems. (Talbot Press, Dublin.)
The Prophet – Kahlil Gibran. (Knopf, N.Y.)
An Anthology of World Poetry – Edited by Mark Van Doren. (Boni, N.Y.)

IV. BOOKS THAT HELP TO UNDERSTAND THE MYSTICAL EXPERIENCE AND ITS SIGNIFICANCE

Mysticism – Evelyn Underhill. (Dutton, N.Y.) Especially Part III: "The Mystic Way."
The Life of the Spirit and the Life of Today – Evelyn Underhill. (Dutton, N.Y.)

The Mysticism of St. Francis – D.H.S. Nicholson. (Small Maynard, Boston.)

**Cosmic Consciousness* – Richard Maurice Bucke. (Dutton, N.Y.)

 *The Art of Creation – Edward Carpenter. (Allen & Unwin, London.)

*A Visit to a Gnani – Edward Carpenter. (Allen & Unwin, London.)

**Tertium Organum – P.D. Ouspensky. (Knopf, N.Y.)

*God – J. Middleton Murry. (Harpers, N.Y.)

V. SOCIAL PROBLEMS

The Revolt of the Masses – Ortega y Gasset. (Norton, N.Y.)

The Modern Theme – Ortega y Gasset. (Norton, N.Y.)

The Decline of the West – Osawld Spengler. (Knopf, N.Y.)

The Hour of Decision – Oswald Spengler. (Knopf, N.Y.)

Mexico – Stuart Chase. (Macmillan, N.Y.) A very interesting contrast of life in a handicraft society with our industrialized society.

This Ugly Civilization – Ralph Borsodi. (Simon & Schuster, N.Y.) A very suggestive study of the machine.

England's Ideal – Edward Carpenter. (Scribners, N.Y.)

Civilization, Its Cause and Cure – Edward Carpenter. (Scribners, N.Y.)

Flight from the City – Ralph Borsodi. (Harpers, N.Y.) Practical suggestions for finding a richer, freer, and more wholesome life than is possible in the mechanized life of our cities.

War – Scott Nearing. (Vanguard Press, N.Y.)

The Dance of Siva – Ananda Coomaraswamy. The chapter entitled "Sahaja." (The Sunwise Turn, Inc., N.Y.) Presents a beautiful sex ideal.

The Remaking of Marriage – Poul Bjerre. (Macmillan, N.Y.)

The Night-Hoers (or the case against Birth Control, and an alternative) – A.M. Ludovici. (Herbert Jenkins, London.)

Man – An Indictment – A.M. Ludovici. (Constable, London.)

Woman – A Vindication – A.M. Ludovici. (Knopf, N.Y.)

VI. MISCELLANEOUS

A New Model of the Universe – P.D. Ouspensky. (Knopf, N.Y.)

A Cultural History of the Modern Age – Egon Friedell. 3 vols. (Knopf, N.Y.)

Stranger than Fiction – Lewis Browne. (Macmillan, N.Y.) A short, vivid sketch of the history of the Jews.

To Jerusalem through the Lands of Islam – Madame Loyson. (Open Court, Chicago.) Most Christians would benefit greatly by reading this book and the one listed next above.

The Nature of the Physical World – A.S. Eddington. (Macmillan, N.Y.)

Fantasia of the Unconscious – D.H. Lawrence. (Martin Secker, London.)

Natural Therapeutics – Henry Lindlahr. (Lindlahr Pub. Co., Chicago.) Vol. I – Philosophy; Vol. II – Practice.

Natural Foods – Otto Carque. (Otto Carque, Los Angeles, Calif.)

www.ingramcontent.com/pod-product-compliance
Lightning Source LLC
Chambersburg PA
CBHW032020090426
42741CB00006B/681